La Familia and
Other Secret Ingredients
to Latinx Student Success

This book is part of the Peter Lang Education list.
Every volume is peer reviewed and meets
the highest quality standards for content and production.

PETER LANG
New York • Bern • Berlin
Brussels • Vienna • Oxford • Warsaw

Jennifer M. Matos

La Familia and
Other Secret Ingredients
to Latinx Student Success

PETER LANG

New York • Bern • Berlin
Brussels • Vienna • Oxford • Warsaw

Library of Congress Cataloging-in-Publication Data

Names: Matos, Jennifer, author.
Title: La familia and other secret ingredients to Latinx student success / Jennifer Matos.
Other titles: Fulfilling their dreams.
Description: New York: Peter Lang, 2019.
Revision of author's thesis (doctoral)—University of Massachusetts Amherst, 2011,
titled Fulfilling their dreams: Latina/o college student narratives on the impact of
parental involvement on their academic engagement.
Includes bibliographical references and index.
Identifiers: LCCN 2019014101 | ISBN 978-1-4331-6720-1 (hardback: alk. paper)
ISBN 978-1-4331-6756-0 (paperback) | ISBN 978-1-4331-6830-7 (ebook pdf)
ISBN 978-1-4331-6831-4 (epub) | ISBN 978-1-4331-6832-1 (mobi)
Subjects: LCSH: Hispanic American children—Education.
Hispanic American parents—United States.
Education—Parent participation—United States.
Academic achievement—United States.
Classification: LCC LC2669 .M37 2019 | DDC 371.829/68073—dc23
LC record available at https://lccn.loc.gov/2019014101
DOI 10.3726/b15695

Bibliographic information published by **Die Deutsche Nationalbibliothek**.
Die Deutsche Nationalbibliothek lists this publication in the "Deutsche
Nationalbibliografie"; detailed bibliographic data are available
on the Internet at http://dnb.d-nb.de/.

© 2019 Peter Lang Publishing, Inc., New York
29 Broadway, 18th floor, New York, NY 10006
www.peterlang.com

To my late mother, Hipolita "Polly" Santiago. This book is the result of your lifelong value of education, your endless belief in me, and your extraordinary love. Everything good that I am, and everything good that I have is because of you. —JMM

Latinx parents, working multiple jobs, helping children whether it's with homework at the kitchen table or on the long journey to the United States, for the ache that comes with what you cannot give, and the dreams you hold for your children. I hope someday we learn to build bridges, and not walls.

TABLE OF CONTENTS

TABLES

ACKNOWLEDGMENTS

This book was being written decades ago in the family kitchen of our shared Jersey City, New Jersey home. I would like to thank my family of origin, Jessie, Annie, and Rosemarie "Gokie" Flores, and although I never got to meet my brother David, as he died before I was born, he is my family, too. My Mother, through all of the obstacles presented by poverty and urban living, managed to raise all of us. Jessie, thank you for being my big brother, calling to check on me, always ready to tell jokes and laugh heartily with me. I am so proud of the man you are, and proud that you are my brother. Annie, you literally saved my life diagnosing me with lupus when you were only fourteen years old! Even though you are my "little" sister, you have been my fiercely loyal protector, and remind me with your playful teasing, not to take myself so seriously. Thank you for always showing up for me. And Gokie. What would I ever have done without you? Your delicious Puerto Rican meals with recipes passed down in our family as well as your strong hugs have always nourished me. When Mom had to be away at work to keep a roof over our heads, you took us to Saturday matinee movies, played with us, and helped with homework. I don't know anyone else as lucky as me to have a cousin, big sister, second mom, and friend.

There are other blessings in our family such as my brother's wife, Marisol (who is always so loving, supportive, and willing to talk) and their daughters Tiffany, and Melissa; Jim, you are a Superman, and I'm so grateful to have someone to giggle and share stories with. Sarah, you were the first one to teach me what it meant to be a parent. Even though I am not your parent, I loved you since the moment I laid eyes on you. I also want to thank the children that came from our small family: Maliya and Anna. I was able to know my maternal grandmother, my abuela Maria Garay, who loved me deeply and who, for me, was Puerto Rico. When I deplane and land at the Luis Muñoz Marin airport in San Juan, I feel as if my face is pressed against my abuela's housecoat like when I would embrace her, and smell the mountains, plantains, and warm Caribbean air. It was a scent I equated with great love. Although I got to meet, but don't remember my paternal grandmother, Ana Ruiz, I carry her in my heart. I feel close to her whenever I say my daughter's name, who was named to honor my grandmother. And I have only met my maternal great-grandmother, my bisabuela Hipolita Montañez Flores, in dreams. I can see her still, with a beautiful dress adorned with brightly colored flowers, and although she never had the chance to tell me so, I know she loved me before I was born, and that loved travelled time and distance to the blood that ran through my Mother's veins, and by inheritance, flows through my veins and pumps my heart. I am honored to have chosen her last name as part of my own.

Growing up, my Mom believed that there were no such things as friends, and that one only had family to rely on. I made it my mission to prove her wrong and hit the jackpot in doing so. I have chosen family in the form of friends and I would like to thank Joy-marie for teaching me how to write a strong resume and for all you taught me about love and acceptance when I needed it most. Samantha, "Miss Wings" and my soul sister, you, Dan, and Bodhi Becker, have welcomed me into your family in such a way that I feel I was born into it. Your friendship and loyalty to me and my success are unprecedented. I love you more than I can say. Jenny, thank you for your unflapping honesty, acceptance of me, and delicious sense of humor. Wayne Schweitzer, you are not only the world's best lupus doctor, you are my dear friend. Franki Nieves, you don't just cut hair, you've seen me through my life's highest highs and lowest lows. Thank you for always listening. Bee Buehring, and Mike Collins, you are walking proof that blood doesn't make a family, love does.

I would also like to thank my "work family" at Mount Holyoke College in the Department of Psychology and Education, with special thanks to Janet

Crosby whose open office door and bright smile are always welcoming, Cheryl McGraw for being a wealth of information and who read my draft, Sandy Lawrence who hired me and was my first guide on this amazing journey at Mount Holyoke, and Kathy Binder. Kathy, you are a tremendous mentor and friend, you have been my champion, and I thank you for "getting me." To my "work brother," Jared Schwartzer, the work I write about that we did in Playita could not have happened without your loyalty, your willingness to dream, and your generous heart. Special thanks to Mari, Avi, and Leora Schwartzer for sharing your Dad with the children of Playita, and for being an important part of this work! Thanks as well to KC Haydon, Mara Breen, and Jennifer Jacoby for your good humor and mentorship, and Sarah Frenette for your decades of friendship and leadership in the education division. And I would be remiss if I didn't thank the rest of my work family: Corey Flanders, John Tawa, Dr. Janelle Gagnon, Nicole Gilbert-Cote, Cheryl Lavigne, Sruti Kanthan, Kelley O'Carroll, Kat Tremblay, Eloise Nimocks, Allegra Corwin-Renner, Katie Byrne, Jamie Church, John Roche, Danielle Godon-Decoteau, Jenessa Seymour, Ahren Fitzroy, Becky Packard, Amber Douglas, Catherine Swift, Ruth Hornsby, Megan Allen, Mike Flynn, Nestor Restrepo, Brian Gadziala, and retired faculty Fran Deutsch, Karen Hollis, Gail Hornstein, Will Millard, and Patty Ramsey. It is truly a gift not only to love the job I have, but to love and admire the people that I work with. Thank you for your endless good humor and support. I owe thanks for the support of Dorothy Mosby and Gary Gillis. I would like to express my gratitude for the collegiality of Liz Markovitz and the apoyo of Vanessa Rosa, David Hernandez, and the NECLS community, as well as the support of NCFDD and Jonnie Orozco and Virajita Singh. Thank you Latrina Denson, Marcella Runell Hall, Annette McDermott and Karen Jacobus. Thanks are extended as well to my Mount Holyoke College students, who are among the best and brightest the world has seen. I would especially like to acknowledge Daisy Reyes, Mari Santiago, Diana Jaramillo, Lessly Portillo, Estefhani Tavarez, Maria Maria Castillo, Emely Minino Soto, Ragini Ghose, and Nicole Granados. Thanks are extended to the Harap family without whom my research in Holyoke could not have been done.

Thank you to Miriam Quiñones, without whom my initial research would not have been possible. I also owe a debt of gratitude to Sonya Stephens, Lenore Reilley, my Irish sister Amy Martin, Jon Western, the whole-hearted parents and community members of the Playita community in San Juan, Puerto Rico, Yulín Cruz, Nilsa Medina, teachers at la Escuela Especializada en Matemáticas, Ciencias y Tecnología (EMCT), Liza and Edgardo Negron, families of Holyoke, Massachusetts, and to my participants—whose important, impactful, and poignant stories I promised to tell. I hope you know how much you shine.

My own teachers provided a wonderful springboard into my future, and to that end, I would like to thank JoAnn Degnan, Mary Lou Lauterhahn, Mary Beth Landis, Debra Canady, and my dear friend, Odalys Diaz. I give thanks for the friendship and mentorship of Catherine Grimes. Catherine, although you are gone, your lessons of compassion and social justice will remain with me, always. My first grade and fourth-grade teachers fostered a love of learning in me and for that, I would like to thank my first-grade teacher, Robin Weaver and my fourth grade teacher, Juliann James.

Thank you to my UMASS Amherst family in the Social Justice Education program who are too many to list here, but who have all been tremendous peers, mentors, and students. Thank you to Sally Campbell Galman. You will always be my chapter three, and I thank you for your constructive feedback and steadfast friendship. Bev Bell, you inspire me and I am so fortunate to be your friend and colleague. Thank you to Mari Casteneda, Laura Valdiviezo, Bailey Jackson, Maurianne Adams, Ximena Zúñiga, Molly Keehn, and Sonia Nieto.

Balance is important in the work of education and social change, and I would like to thank Ashley Kohl, Loryn Englebrecht, and my Thursday night tap dance class at Ohana.

To Ita Ford, M.M., Maura Clarke, M.M., Dorothy Kazel, O.S.U., and Jean Donovan, your courage, love, and ultimate sacrifice for the marginalized has been a call to me to work for social justice and to serve as a voice for the voiceless.

Thank you to Janell Harris, Patty Mulrane, Monica Baum, and the team at Peter Lang Publishing for all of your support and enthusiasm from the moment I submitted my proposal. Thank you for recognizing the importance of Latinx voices.

Tash, you are everything. Thank you for not giving up on me, for your kindness and generosity, for deep conversations and endless fits of laughter, for the gifts of Quincy and Emmylou, and for the brilliant future that awaits us! I don't know how I'll do it, but I'll work hard to be worthy of you.

Anna, you are an amazing daughter, and I loved you since before you were born. It is my privilege and greatest joy to be your parent. You teach me so much about love and life every day and you are my buddy. I hope that this book gives you insight into why I parent you around education in the way that I do.

Finally, I would like to thank my Mother for the many sacrifices she made for the sake of my education. While Mom did not get to see me become an author of a book, she got to see me become "Dr. Matos" and this is a distinction from which she derived great pride. Mom, having you as my parent is something from which I consistently derive great pride. I am proud to be your child, and I hope you are as proud of me as I am of you.

ABBREVIATIONS

DOE	Department of Education
EMCT	Escuela Especializada en Matemáticas, Ciencias y Tecnología
ESEA	Elementary and Secondary Education Act
FAFSA	Free Application for Federal Student Aid
FP	Frances Perkins Scholars
FTM	Female to male
GED	General Education Diploma
GRE	Graduate Record Examinations
GNC	Gender Non-Conforming
HCC	Holyoke Community College
IEP	Individualized Education Plan
MAT	Miller Analogies Test
MHC	Mount Holyoke College
M.P.F.	Maestre Pie Filippini
NCES	National Center for Education Statistics
NCLB	No Child Left Behind
PTA	Parent Teacher Association
PWI	Predominantly White Institution
SASS	School and Staffing Survey

SAT	Scholastic Aptitude Test
SSSP	Smith Summer Science Program
STEM	Science, Technology, Engineering, and Math
UMASS	University of Massachusetts

· 1 ·

INTRODUCTION

My educational trajectory started, as many of life's beginnings do, with a Mother. In this case, my life-long career in education started with my Mother. A native of Caguas, Puerto Rico, Mom wasn't able to complete her education when she came to the mainland United States in the 1950's. The story of my family is the typical immigrant story with the exception that legally, Puerto Ricans are also United States citizens. However, when a Puerto Rican moves to the mainland U.S., it's not the same as when someone on the mainland moves from Pennsylvania to Florida. Having the greatest grasp of the English language, my ten-year-old Mother had to accompany my grandmother from apartment building to apartment building in search of affordable housing for four people. As my Mom was the one doing the translating, she was also the one bearing the brunt of racist epithets that potential landlords lobbed at her as they slammed the door in her face. She learned quickly that she and her family weren't ever to receive a warm welcome in this country and as she fumed, my grandmother urged her to calm down, not understanding what her young daughter was learning. While she completed a GED, she always seemed to live vicariously through my education. When I was a small child, she would say "Jennifer, you're going to go to school until you have gray hair!" I remember thinking I would be *very old* by the time I finished school. This directive was later replaced by "You're going to college—I can't pay for it—but you're going." As a single parent, she worked two, sometimes three jobs as a certified nursing assistant in hospitals and nursing homes to fund my sister's and my Catholic school education. She thought we would be safer and receive a better education in a Catholic school and sent us despite my father's unwillingness to pay for any of it. I was forced to go to my high school senior prom because she never had the opportunity to attend high school and go to her own prom. Understanding what my attendance would mean to her, I agreed to get my hair and nails done, have my cousin apply makeup to my face, and wear a gown. Looking back, I could have done without all the fuss, but it meant the world to my Mom to witness me having the full high school experience. She endured relentless criticism by extended family who claimed she was being "stuck up" and "acting white" by sending us to private schools. She persisted. Throughout her life, even though she didn't have a "formal" education, she believed that it offered a magical key to a door that blocked entrances and opportunities for her. Having identified what she believed to be the key to success, she desperately wanted to place it in our hands.

Being raised poor, and having little resources, we worked at the kitchen table, not a desk; we had pencils Mom sharpened with a knife, making our Dixon Ticonderoga #2 pencils look like tiny trees, as a pencil sharpener would make an appearance later in our lives. Since she could not afford the entire Grolier's Encyclopedia set all at once, my sister and I would have to painfully pore over one volume at a time until she could afford the next installment. One year for Christmas, she gifted us with blue and white typewriters because she knew we loved to write. I remember using *both sides* of every piece of paper I could get my hands on to write stories and poems. The last day of school was the worst day for me as while other children were chanting "no more pencils…!" I could be found sobbing inconsolably in the school's parking lot. I would rummage through the school trash for unfinished workbooks and half used notebooks that had been tossed away by carefree students. I loved school, and it was all my Mother's fault, really because education was the only world I ever knew, and it was what my Mother revealed to me. Mom would work late night shifts and arrive back home while my sister and I carefully slipped the Catholic school uniforms over our heads. There were only two uniforms for each of us as the cost was exorbitant, so we had to be very careful not to soil what we had. This type of "secret survival" is what so many first-generation students of color I've interviewed and worked with, have experienced. The last thing I needed was for someone to fabricate a prediction of my worth that did not match my potential, and my Mother knew that, so she anticipated obstacles and prepared us for them.

I remember walking down the stairs in the direction of my breakfast cereal to find my math workbook in its company, conveniently opened to the page with an unfinished math problem. I could feel the burning in my cheeks as I anticipated the inevitable lecture and Spanish inquisition that would follow. "Why isn't this done?! You have to finish what you started!" and "Your book cover is dirty! Your name is on that—if your name is on something, it has to be clean!" Not only did my work have to be impeccable, my work had to be *immaculate*. My name on inferior or unclear work was a statement of collusion, and my Mother would have none of it. It was more than protection of my reputation. My Mother understood that as someone who inhabited a female body, and a body of color, that I had several strikes against me, and she knew as she would warn us *"do you know what they think about Puerto Ricans?!,"* that we would always have to work twice as hard and be twice as good than our white peers. She pushed us in school, and she pushed *hard*.

"Report card" day was a dreaded day for me, as I would hand my report card to my Mother who would look over every grade and whether or not it had risen or fallen. Occasionally, she'd peer over the card to look at me, and I endured the inquisition again. "This was a B+, why is it a B?" These weren't questions she actually expected me to answer as I had no defense. In the last quarter of the eighth grade, I handed her a report card with something she had not seen in the eight years prior—it was a report card bursting at the crease with A's and A+'s. I remember puffing my chest out a little as I handed it to her and remember thinking "She can't say *anything* about this one." She took the card and peered over it occasionally, before saying "Why aren't these *all* A+s?" I'd like to think she was kidding, but I know better.

Despite wanting to run away from home and join a circus for academic underachievers, I did very well in high school and gained admission to Smith College in Northampton, Massachusetts. I didn't know Smith College had existed before Sr. Margaret, my English teacher approached the boys in my class to see if they wanted to attend the Smith Summer Science Program. Sr. Margaret's nephew was a professor at Smith, and he had sent her a flyer that she was now circulating to my male peers. I remember glowering at the boys and wishing that I could have a summer in Massachusetts, studying science at a college. When she realized that Smith was a women's college,[1] she approached the girls. The program was in its pilot year, and I immediately started filling out the forms and completing the essay. I would later be shown the essay I had written in 1990, and I could not believe my eyes. I had written about how I eventually wanted to be a Flight Surgeon for the United States Navy, and how I intended on being the best one. Not knowing my audience, I was totally speaking to the Smith College mission for women's education and excellence. I never told my Mom that I was applying to the program. In my teenage brain, I decided that I didn't need to tell her I was *applying*, I only needed to tell her if I got in. That spring, a large white envelope addressed to me was mailed to my home. I got in. Then my teenage brain rationalized that I only needed to tell her I got in if I won the scholarship I applied for. When I received word that I had secured a full scholarship to the month-long program, it was time to fess up. I had momentarily considered not telling her at all, demurring and writing back to the SSSP to say "thanks, but no thanks" and keeping the secret of what I had attempted to do. But I knew that attending the Smith Summer Science Program was something I had to do. Not only did I get a full scholarship, I was also placed in my top-pick of classes, a biology course where I would study newts, and a psychology course where I would learn about the theories of racism. So, I swallowed hard, and marched up to my unsuspecting Mother. I had to listen to the rapid-fire Spanish she spoke when she was really angry, but it subsided once I explained that I was going to a college, and that it was all "girls," and that it could help me when it was time to apply to colleges. None of us had any idea what Smith College actually was. How could we?

On the first day of the program, my family drove me to Northampton, and my Mom wore a pink dress and heels while other parents were casually dressed in shorts, t-shirts, and tennis shoes. After all, this was a summer camp, but it was still a college and no one in my family had ever gone away to a camp or to a college. This would be one of the earlier lessons about being first-generation. I immediately fell in love with the campus with its gardens, ponds, and Gothic-style buildings. I was in awe of the fact that I would spend the month with a house full of girls, who like me, were good students and loved to learn. The resources available at the College were unlike anything I had ever seen. Summer participants would be working with multi-million-dollar equipment and when we were asked to provide a list of materials we needed to conduct our experiments, we got everything on our list. This was a stark contrast to what I was used to in my own education. Earlier that year in my biology class, Mr. McDonough had wanted to have us perform dissections on frogs. The problem was that we didn't have any frogs to dissect, and purchasing such items was not in our school budget. One afternoon while cleaning, Mr. Mc-

Donough found a bucket of frogs deep within the biology supply closet. The bucket was from the 1960s, but since they were in formaldehyde, Mr. McDonough said they could be used. I still remember the smell as I walked into the cafeteria to identify the internal parts of a frog for our exam. Since there weren't enough frogs for all sections of biology to dissect, and since there was a steep economic price for any errors, Mr. McDonough had dissected the few frogs himself. At Smith, the leaders were all college-aged women who would be mentors and like big sisters. I was in love with the campus, but I also had to adjust to the culture shock. Compared to the residents of Jersey City, the residents of Northampton were extremely friendly, with their good morning greetings and wishes for me to have a nice day. Falling asleep on the quiet campus, and without the background sounds of garbage trucks, speeding cars and city busses, was a challenge that would take quite some time to overcome. I was homesick for about the first half of the program, and then it would be time for me to recreate the scene from the last day of school, inconsolable and in tears. After completing the program, I decided not only that I wanted to go to Smith College, I *needed* to go.

I was the first person to go to college, and again, my Mother had to endure the criticism of her family "only white people kick their kids out of the house." As my extended family would try to dress me down by charging me with the offense of "acting white" for reading and loving school, they were also penalizing my Mother for the audacity to support my admission to college. As a first-generation student of color at a highly selective college, everything was a challenge for me from reading the menus ("what's gnocchi?") to buying books and watching parents write $10,000 checks for their daughters to give them "pocket change" while I earned $60 a week from my work-study job. When I feared the price of books or the meeting I would have with the bursar, I would call Mom for a pep talk. Those talks spurred me on and reminded me of the finish line. My family had never attended a college graduation, and they experienced a bit of culture shock as we walked past college houses toward the Quad with parking lots adorned with brand new cars awaiting their new owners. My Mother apologized for not being in the financial position to purchase a brand-new car for me. She sat with my family as she watched the procession of faculty and dignitaries invited to participate in the ceremony, and later had questions about the colorful robes and the "funny hats." I was absolutely in love with being a college student, so I had studied academic regalia and informed my Mother that the color of the robes signified where the professor had attended college, and the color of their hoods was indicative of their field of study. As for the "funny hats," I explained that they were called "tams" and part of doctoral academic regalia. Her next fixation was on when I would get one of the "funny hats."

As family members took their daughters to lunch after Commencement, my Mother offered to buy me a sandwich from Subway. Through lunch, she seemed to be absorbing the enormity of not only what she had just witnessed, but hopefully, what she had also made possible. When I graduated from Smith College (again) with my Master of Arts in Teaching, my family was ready, throwing a graduation party with a traditional Puerto Rican meal. While the graduation menu had changed, my Mother's continued interrogation about the schedule for the "funny hat" did not. Three years after graduating from my master's program, I gained admission to the Social Justice Education doctoral program at the University of Massachusetts at Amherst. Students aren't the only ones in education who experience being first-generation; families have a parallel experience and also have to learn new vocabulary and ways of being. Unfortunately, sometimes education creates a chasm when it should create a bridge, and families can get lost in that terrain. I knew that all I had to tell Mom about my doctoral application process was that I was going after the "funny hat," and I also added that I would be *done with school after this!* The fact that her child would attain the highest educational degree possible, that I would be "Dr. Matos" was something that made Mom puff out her chest as I had done when I handed her my eighth grade report card. During the five years it took me to complete my degree, Mom would call to make sure that I had eaten breakfast before classes "you know you can't learn on an empty stomach," she would advise. When I questioned my pluck to be able to become a Doctor of Education, her "¡si se puede!" attitude kept me going. The graduation party outdid the master's degree party, and I wore my rented regalia for her for the duration. At the end of the day, I took the funny hat off of my head, and tenderly placed it in her hands.

"This is yours. You earned it." I said.

My story of having a single parent Latina Mother who was invested in and dedicated to my education is not unique. I learned this as I was conducting a pilot study with Latina students. Story after story, I heard about a mother or a father who gave up a professional career in another country, so their daughter could have an education in the United States. I heard about dreaded report card days where mothers scrutinized every letter and every point. I heard about students being cheered on in their educational careers by blood and extended families. I heard about families who could not get their children to school but utilized the Latinx[2] social network to make magic happen. I heard about education creating an abyss and sat with participants as we both tried to figure out how to traverse that landscape. The question that arose in my researcher's mind was "why?" Why was it that my story from 40 years ago in New Jersey and emerging stories from students from Colombia, the Dominican Republic, El Salvador, Mexico, Boston, Texas, California and beyond, were not being told?

Despite the booming Latinx population in the United States, as I will describe further in this chapter, there exists a master narrative fabricated from fear and disseminated through stereotypes that Latinxs are responsible for their own social ills. These falsehoods suggest that they possess deficits in their desire to strive for upward mobility and are deficient in their family values, and lacking in social capital. Additionally, this story excuses the system of oppression in creating inequality and scapegoats Latinx families. I have seen this in the literature on Latinx parents, and I have witnessed it first-hand as a high school teacher. Colleagues would bemoan low attendance rates at open houses and would be unabashed in claiming "those parents just don't care" and then stare wide-eyed at my classroom, all abuzz with Latinx parents and caregivers, grandparents, and siblings. "Those parents," you see, had been called at home, with news of praise I shared over their child's accomplishments. The good grade, the improved grade, the helpfulness, the leadership, was all described to them, without a subscription to the belief that there were "those" kids and "good" kids. All parents and caregivers were members of my community. All students were *my* students.

Research Studies

As you will see in the pages that follow in this book, there is not one way to be a student, nor is there one way to be a parent. This book provides background on the notion of parental engagement, as well as the how and why of how Latinx parental engagement is viewed and valued differently when compared to white parental engagement. More than anything, this book is a collection of stories in two-parts with narratives from Latinx college students and narratives from Latinx parents.

Dissertation Research

My dissertation research was collected in two steps. First, I conducted a pilot study at a private women's college in the Northeast. I wanted to understand what Latinx parental engagement looked like for other Latinx academics. I had believed that my Mother's parenting strategies of book bag searches and obsession over education was unique to her. As I conducted semi-structured interviews with members of the Latina organization on campus, I soon realized that I was learning not of exclusive parenting styles, but of a phenomenon in Latinx parental engagement in education. One participant shared that her parents drugged her and her sister, hid them in the spare tire compartment of the family car and crossed the border. When I asked what would have possessed her parents to go to such extremes, she told me that her parents knew they could get a better education in the United States. Another shared how her parents held advanced degrees and were professionals in their country of origin, making good money and enjoying the status and privileges that come with professional careers, and abandoning that so that she could have a better education in the United States. As I listened to each story, I wondered how it was possible that women from Texas, Illinois, Massachusetts, California, New York, and New Jersey shared stories similar to mine. My curiosity begged me to further understand how these narratives were not a part of the national dialogue on parental engagement. This led me to my dissertation research.

For the pilot study, I used a private women's college as the research site, and I went in merely wanting to know what their parents taught them about education. After reading "Whose Culture has Capital?" by Tara Yosso, I learned about six forms of capital transmitted by Latinx parents to their children.

1. Aspirational capital is described as a form of capital that encourages children to hold on to their hopes and dreams despite obstacles, and is expressed in its "¡Si se puede" attitude.
2. Familial capital is manifested in connections with family and extended family.
3. Linguistic capital is sometimes viewed as a deficit in schools, bit is actually an asset as students employ storytelling and utilization of memorization, attention to detail, dramatic pauses, comedic timing, facial affect, vocal tone, volume, rhythm and rhyme.
4. Navigational capital pertains to fortifying children with inner resources and resilience that empower their children to endure stressful events and hostile environments.

5. Resistance capital is explained as lessons that teach children the skills of oppositional behavior to challenge inequality.
6. Social capital utilizes social networks to obtain resources needed for their children to experience positive educational outcomes.

Armed with this new knowledge, I was curious to see what forms of capital (if any) Latinx students decided to bring with them. In my years of wearing different hats in student affairs positions, I knew that some students took their presence at a college as an opportunity to shed what they had learned at home to reinvent themselves. I remember when I returned home from college for the first big holiday break, my announcement that I now liked tofu and was trying to be a vegetarian created quite the scandal. A refusal to eat meat—especially during a family holiday—was as close to treason as I dared to get.

In my capacities as an Area Coordinator, Associate Director of Residence Life, Director of Multicultural Affairs, Assistant Dean of Students, Advisor to Latinx Students, and college course instructor, I worked with college students in many different capacities and had a front-row seat to how they changed from timid first years to bold seniors and became their own people in the process. If Latinx parents transmitted capital as Yosso suggested, how much did that capital "stick" once the children left home?

I wanted my dissertation research to be as comprehensive as possible, and so I decided to examine this question at different educational sites. Data were collected from three educational institutions in the Northeast: a selective all-women's college, a community college, and a large university. I recruited participants for this study by reaching out to personal contacts at the three institutions and recruited college students who were at least second semester first year students and older, who identified as Latinx, and who were raised by a Latinx parent or caretaker. I held three focus groups (one at each institution) and conducted over 30 individual interviews across all three sites. Individual interviews were 90-minute semi-structured interviews. Each research site and subsequent findings from those sites are further described in chapters five, six, and seven.

The whole process was emotional and deeply personal to me as much of what participants shared with me resonated with my own experience as a life-long learner and as a Latinx-identified person. Participants laughed through interviews, some cried and had to pause to collect themselves. The interviews also exhausted me as story after story I had to bear witness to hope in the face of a dire and relentless system of oppression, while recalling my own story. I remember sitting straight up in bed one night, frustrated with the dissertation and data collection process, feeling like I didn't need to subject myself to this academic hazing, that I was smart enough to just find a job that I didn't have to take home, and that would pay me well. I asked my spouse at the time, to help me understand why I had chosen to torture myself. She reminded me that I had wanted to get a doctorate, and that it had been a long-standing dream of mine to secure the highest educational degree possible. I replied that those reasons were not enough for me to go to sleep at 10 pm and wake up at 3 am every day, to write, to teach, to collect data, and repeat. After thinking for a moment, I turned to her and said, "No, that's not it. I promised them all that I would tell *their* stories. *I promised.*" With that, I shoved the covers off of my body, pulled on a sweatshirt and went to my study to keep my promise.

The stories that emerge from this first data set that I have collected come from college student participants who shared the social capital they learned from their parents, and how those lessons manifest in college. Within these narratives, students shared two additional forms of capital (replication of familial capital and "finishing") that provide depth to the paths their parents' sacrifices started them on and show just how powerful Latinx stories are. They shared stories about their afterschool routines and the messages received and lessons learned from their parents regarding education. What I found to be particularly fascinating was that since my dissertation was published in August of 2011, it has been downloaded almost 800 times from places like Amsterdam, Turkey, Greece, Tanzania, Ghana, South Africa, Pakistan, Moscow, the Philippines, China, the United Kingdom, Germany, Ethiopia, the Netherlands, and Australia to Texas, Colorado, California, New York, New Jersey, Connecticut, Illinois, Alabama, Florida, Mississippi, and beyond, and it has been downloaded by governmental, educational, health, and commercial organizations in the U.S.. Upon seeing the readership that my published dissertation had, I wanted to put this information in the hands of more people to be more accessible, and the information contained within to be as helpful as possible, to as many as possible. With this goal in mind, I approached Peter Lang Publishing with my book proposal.

Post-Doctoral Research

The dissertation research process fully immersed me in the narratives of Latinx college students and cultural capital. Now, as researchers are apt to do, I have a new research question. If Latinx parents from different Latinx ethnicities share similar parenting strategies regarding education, is it possible that the Latinx value for education is an inherent trait? Initial findings on that topic will be discussed later in this book. Having updated my doctoral research since 2011, I worked with Mount Holyoke College students Mari Santiago, Daisy Reyes, Emely Minino Soto, Nicole Lara Granados, Maria Maria Castillo, Estefhani Tavarez, and Julia Montiel on collecting data from Puerto Rican parents in Holyoke, Massachusetts and a barrio called Playita in San Juan, Puerto Rico. The data collection process for the new research sites is reviewed again in chapter eight. I would also like to add that data collection from my doctoral research as well as the Massachusetts and Puerto Rico sites disproportionately represents cisgender Latina women. While I employed various recruitment tactics, time and again, women were the ones responding to the calls for participants. I do not largely refer to this group as Latinas, but instead use *Latinx* a controversial and relatively new term that is gender inclusive and does not conform to the notion of a gender binary. I realize that not all readers might be comfortable or supportive of the inclusion of this designation, however, in the interest of gender inclusivity, I have chosen this option.

To recruit participants in Holyoke, Mari and Daisy used their personal networks and connections within the Holyoke Public School system to advertise the study and gain access to participants. Through the generosity of the Harap Family and Harap fund available to student researchers at Mount Holyoke College (MHC) and recognizing that Latinx narratives have traditionally been exploited and appropriated, we were able to compensate each participant with a small amount of cash, and food and transportation to the focus group event. Mari recruited and interviewed parents who had children in high school, and Daisy recruited and interviewed parents who had children in elementary and middle schools. The individual interviews were 90-minute semi-structured interviews that took place in locations familiar and accessible to parents in Holyoke. Both Mari and Daisy facilitated the focus group.

Emely and Nicole called parents in Playita, who were listed as primary contacts for student participants in a Mount Holyoke College sponsored Science Technology Engineering and Math (STEM) program in the summer of 2018.[3] They acquired verbal consent for participation over the phone and conducted semi-structured interviews. Questions covered messages that parents had received about education from their own parents, their post-school routines, and expectations regarding homework and school performance. Parents were also asked about the messages they impart to their children, what they believe to be the role of the classroom teacher, and how they feel that they support the teacher while the student is at home. Parents in Holyoke were also asked these questions, however, the questions that the Playita parents were asked differed in that they were first asked about their general impressions of the summer program. Unfortunately, I was not able to secure funding nor was there a reasonable way to compensate Playita parents. Data will also be collected in person in Playita in the summer of 2019, at which time I hope to be able to offer participants monetary compensation for their time. Interview questions were asked by Emely, and Nicole transcribed the responses. Coordinating interviews off site and at such a distance served as a disadvantage. Under other circumstances, I would have requested a virtual conference call, however, many of the families we worked with in Playita do not have access to home computing systems, and some do not have internet access or support with operating web conferencing systems.

This book does not claim that all Latinx families are involved or invested in education, just as not all white parents are involved or invested in education. Merely, it establishes a pattern and way of being that is a common thread in the literature and my research. Additionally, this book is not intended to be a quick remedy for educators and administrators who might feel that in reading this, they can check off the "diversity" box. This book is intended to begin a dialogue and does not tell you about all Latinx families. I have done my best to make this book accessible, and not filled with terminology that perpetuates an academic divide. I struggled between using jargon and furthering a stereotype that Latinx people don't possess the intellectual curiosity to deepen their own learning. My own Mother carried a pocketbook-sized dictionary with her until the day she died, and I know that the Latinx desire to learn doesn't end with her.

The discovery of the strengths, brilliance, and warmth of Latinx students and the people who love and care for them, is a life-long discovery and I welcome you in this journey.

Latinxs in U.S. Education

For the first four years of my life, I thought that I was Italian. We lived on the corner of Fourth and Monmouth Streets in Jersey City, New Jersey, which was an Italian neighborhood. My Spanish-speaking Mother would speak to Victoria Romaniello in Spanish, and she'd respond in Italian, and they understood each other. I thought they were speaking the same language. In school, I would learn to dance the tarantella, and I knew all of the words to "Tu Scendi

Dalle Stelle," and I would sing to the Italian women on our block, one hand on my chest and the other arm outstretched, with my eyes always closed because I was *feeling it*. The Italian women would give me crisp one-dollar bills and pinch my fluffy cheeks. Hard. I was taught my ABCs by Theresa Sutter, the paraplegic woman we lived with. Taking care of her daily needs served as rent paid by my Mother and cousin, "Gokie." I called Theresa "Tessie" and she would allow me to sit with her in her room while "All My Children" was on in the background. I was only allowed to speak during commercials. In between the trials and tribulations of the people of "Pine Valley" and the romantic escapades of Erica Kane, she taught me the alphabet. My Mother was a seamstress and would sew for a man named Lenny who owned a factory in Hoboken. If my education was volleyball, Tessie served the ball and Mom hit it over the net. I remember my Mother fussing over me one sunny morning because we had to meet Sr. Irma Papaleo, M.P.F., the Principal of the Holy Rosary School, which was only a few blocks away. "The nun is going to give you a test," Mom said as she fixed my collar. "And if you pass the test, you can start kindergarten this year."

I remember how the foyer of the school smelled like it had been freshly mopped. My Mother held my hand as we climbed the shiny staircase that led to the third floor. After announcing ourselves to Ann Piazza, the secretary, I was led—alone—to the office of Sr. Irma. I don't remember her being particularly warm, but I do remember that this test seemed like a big deal.

"Which way is up?" I lifted my chubby cheeks to the sky as she gave the next set of instructions. "Which way is down?" I dropped my head down and stared at a sunny spot on the floor. "Show me your right hand." I raised my right hand. "Show me your left hand." I lifted my left hand. "Mmm hmm" she said cryptically while she wrote something down in her notebook, closed it, and opened the door to the room where my Mother had been waiting. Mom seemed relieved when Sr. Irma announced that I could start kindergarten in the fall. I was four years old.

In the present-day, children have technology and apps and they seem to know their ABCs, but in the days before the Internet and before televisions had remote controls, it seemed that the alphabet was something you learned in school. My kindergarten teacher was Sr. Grace De Mundo, M.P.F., a round woman with thick eyeglass lenses. As she used her pointer to direct our attention to each letter of the alphabet, my hand shot up like a rocket. After all, the alphabet was already an old friend. I was told to stop raising my hand because it would make the other kids feel bad. Eight years later, I was told that the school had decided that I would share the scholarship I had won with the smartest white boy in class so he wouldn't "feel bad." Now I find myself wondering what it would have been like if the school allowed the smartest student to be Puerto Rican.

Latinxs and Institutional Discrimination

The first lessons I learned about racism I learned forty years ago, at the age of four. Girls I considered to be friends would tell me "I'm not allowed to have Puerto Ricans at my house. But my mom says it's ok for you to come over because you're not like *those* Puerto Ricans." If parents were harboring racist sentiments, I shudder to think what the teachers thought of me. Teachers are human beings, and human beings are socialized by the people who care for us, and for better or worse, they teach us what they know. Anti-Latinx sentiments scar the history of this Country with stories of colonization, violence, and segregation with stereotypes used as systemic justification for racial oppression. Just as Irish immigrants were met with "no Irish need apply" signs, Mexicans faced signs that read "no dogs or Mexicans allowed in this restaurant." Puerto Ricans also faced sentiments that furthered racial animus with signs that read "no blacks, no dogs, no Puerto Ricans" (Mitchell, 2014). Between 1930–1960, the United States government addressed the issue of "overpopulation" of Puerto Ricans by sterilizing Puerto Rican women without their knowledge or consent in what Puerto Rican women referred to as "*la operación*" (Acosta-Belén & Santiago, 2018). In 1931, during the period of the Great Depression, immigration agents accosted Mexican-Americans— regardless of citizenship status—and deported them to Mexico. People with Mexican heritage were seen as stealing jobs from Americans, and 2 million Mexican-Americans were deported at the end of 1936 (Blakemore, 2017). Mexican-Americans were barred from sitting in a movie theater anywhere except the balcony and were prohibited from using public swimming pools on weekends when they were being used by white people. They were allowed access to public swimming facilities on Mondays, after which time pools were drained and refilled for white patrons. (Echavarri & Bishop, 2016). Schools were also segregated, and before the infamous *Brown v. The Board of Education* case that ruled school segregation based on race was unconstitutional, there was *Mendez v. Westminster*. During the two-week-long Mendez case, school officials attempted to provide a rationale for racial segregation in Orange County Schools by saying "Latino students were dirty and infected with diseases that put students at risk." One school official said that "Mexicans are inferior in personal hygiene, ability, and in their economic outlook" (Blakemore, 2017). The *Mendez v. Westminster* class action lawsuit ended de jure segregation in California in 1947 and paved the way for *Brown v. Board of Education* in 1954 as some of the arguments used to win Brown were used in the Mendez case.

While landmark cases have ended segregation in schools, U.S. public schools are still segregated, and racist sentiments, policies, and practices, have profound effects on Latinx students. According to a 2015 Pew Research Center report, approximately 56.6% of Latinxs were reported living in the U.S. (Pew Research Center, 2016), and half of second generation Latinxs are bilingual (Pew Research Center, 2015). In 2016, 52% of Latinxs surveyed by the Pew Research Center reported that they had experienced racial discrimination (Pew Research Center, 2016).

Current Statistics on Latinxs in the United States

According to U.S. Census Data, as of July 1, 2017, 58.9 million Latinxs resided in the United States, making them 18.1% of the nation's total population. The U.S. Census reported that as of July 1, 2016, 57.5 million Latinxs resided in the U.S. creating a 2% increase between 2015 and 2016. In this time frame, 1,131,766 million Latinxs were added to the U.S. population that accounted for more than half of the country's 2.2 million people added during this time frame. By the year 2060, at 119 million people projected, Latinxs will make up 28.6% of the nation's population. In 2016, the U.S. Census reported that 40 million U.S. residents aged 5 years and older spoke Spanish at home, which is a 133.4% increase since 1990. Latinx students enrolled in kindergarten through 12th grade made up 24.7% of the population, and 17.4% of Latinxs accounted for both undergraduate and graduate level enrollment. According to the National Center for Education Statistics 2017 Report, "between fall 2003 and fall 2013, the percentage of students enrolled in public elementary and secondary schools decreased for students who were white (from 59% to 50%) and Black (from 17% to 16%). In contrast, the percentage increased for students who were Hispanic (from 19% to 25%) and Asian/Pacific Islander (from 4% to 5%) during the same time period." By 2025, Latinx students will account for 29% of students enrolled in pre-kindergarten through 12th grade (NCES, 2017).

The fact that the Latinx population in the U.S. continues to boom is unrefuted, but what has to be addressed is how to adequately care for, educate, and support this rising population. The Latinx student population is still grossly disproportionate to the resources they have to succeed. Over time, Latinx students are making progress in mathematics and literacy, but so are white students, meaning that the "achievement gap" isn't narrowing. In 2016, the National Center for Education Statistics reported that the Latinx student dropout rate was 9.1% compared to an overall dropout rate of 5.8% (NCES, 2016). Possible reasons for Latinx dropout rates are the hostile environments that Latinx students inhabit while in educational settings. Researchers at the University of Texas at Austin and the University of California at Los Angeles wanted to examine how discrimination affected school performance, particularly school attendance and grades. In 2011 they published a study in *Child Development*. This published work, "Latino Adolescents' Experiences of Discrimination Across the First Two Years of High School: Correlates and Influences on Educational Outcomes" utilized collected data from 668 Latinx student questionnaires. Student participants were in the ninth and tenth grades. One of the findings of the study found that "greater levels of discrimination and sharper increases in discrimination were associated with poorer perceptions of school climate at the end of 10th grade; this perception of school climate was found to be a predictor of students' grade point averages and total absences at the end of 10th grade." Researchers also stated that "experiences with discrimination are recognized as a major stressor that can take their toll on physical and mental health of ethnic minority youth as well as adults" (Benner & Graham, 2011).

Research on teacher perceptions of Latinx students is also deeply troubling. Teachers given the kindergarten Early Childhood Longitudinal Study (ECLS) were asked to assess the proficiency and readiness of their students in math and literacy. According to Reardon and Galindo (2003), regardless of student academic aptitude, teachers rated Latinx students lower than white students. Research by Finn (1989) shows a connection between students' sense of belonging and connection within their schools. Students who experienced an internal sense of belonging were more likely to participate in school. Payne (1994) and Valenzuela (1999) found that negative teacher perceptions and stereotypes had an adverse effect on a student's capacity for learning. They found that respect and a demonstration for student learning was related to student academic success. Mexican American students felt relief when they were not with their teachers who they believed harbored disparaging sentiments about them (Martinez, 2003). Teacher bias is a contributing factor to Latinx student detachment, and when a Latinx student feels that their teach-

er, the person primarily responsible for assessing their work and determining their value, neither respects nor cares for them, student ability to realize
the importance of their academic work is impacted (Schneider, Martinez, &
Owens, 2006). Additionally, Latinx public school teachers are grossly under-
represented in the teaching profession. The 2007–2008 Schools and Staffing
Survey (SASS) reports that Latinx teachers make up only 7% of the teaching
workforce in public schools and 6% of the teaching force in private schools
(NCES, 2007).

If hostile environments and teacher bias are some of the contributing factors for Latinx dropout rates and student disengagement, what can be done
to keep Latinx students in school? I argue that there exists an underutilized
resource in Latinx student academic achievement. In the pages of this book,
I assert that *la familia*—the network of blood related and extended family—is
the secret ingredient for Latinx student academic success. Current national
discourse regarding Latinxs echoes Great Depression-era rhetoric of Latinxs
as lazy and dangerous interlopers threatening to steal American jobs. Depor-
tations and incarcerations of Latinx peoples are alive and well, as are crimes
against Latinxs. According to an NPR story, hate crimes against Latinxs rose
by more than 50% in the State of California alone in 2016 (Hinojosa, 2018).
Disparaging and racist stereotypes regarding Latinxs abound in the current
day and Latinxs are viewed and regarded from a deficit perspective. This book
holds as its analytic framework, deficit theory, Critical Race Theory (CRT),
Latino Critical Race Theory (LatCrit), and culture of wealth theory. To make
the contents of this book accessible and useful to as large an audience as possible, I will explain these analytical frameworks in the following chapters. I
will also explain the assets that Latinx students and families bring to educational spaces and why those contributions are invisible. As this book is about
familia—the secret ingredient in Latinx academic resilience and success, I
will begin by explaining parental engagement to provide a common understanding and vocabulary to facilitate a dialogue from this book. I will also explain how Latinx parents understand and manifest parental engagement and
why those contributions are invisible. Data collected and analyzed from my
research with Latinx college students will be discussed. Their voices illumi-
nate the contributions and importance of familia in college academic success.
I will also share new data from studies conducted with parents in Holyoke,
Massachusetts and the barrio of Playita in San Juan, Puerto Rico. Finally, I
will share suggestions for practical applications of concepts in this book to the
areas of education and educational administration.

Notes

1. Smith College is a gender inclusive college that also admits transgender men.
2. Author's choice to use Latinx, a more gender inclusive version of Latina/o.
3. This program is described in further detail in Chapter 8.

References

Acosta-Belén, E., & Santiago, C. E. (2018). *Puerto Ricans in the United States: A contemporary portrait.* (2nd ed.). London: Lynne Rienner.

Benner, A. D., & Graham, S. (March-April 2011). Latino adolescents' experiences of discrimination across the first two years of high school: Correlates and influences on educational outcomes. *Child Development, 82*(2), 508–519.

Blakemore, E. (2017, September 27). The brutal history of anti-Latino discrimination in America. *History.* Retrieved from https://www.history.com/news/the-brutal-history-of-anti-latino-discrimination-in-america

Echavarri, F., & Bishop, M. (Hosts). (2016, March 11). "No Mexicans Allowed": School segregation in the Southwest [Radio broadcast episode]. https://www.npr.org/2016/03/11/470095873/no-mexicans-allowed-school-segregation-in-the-southwest

Finn, D. J. (1989). Withdrawing from school. *Review of Educational Research, 59*(2), 117–142.

Hinojosa, M. (Host). (2018, July 15). Hate crimes against Latinos increase in California [Radio broadcast episode]. https://www.npr.org/2018/07/15/629212976/hate-crimes-against-latinos-increase-in-california

Martinez, S. (2003). *Explaining patterns of disengagement of Mexican Americans in high school.* (Unpublished doctoral dissertation). University of Chicago, Chicago, IL.

Mitchell, P. R. (2014). *History of Latinos: Exploring diverse roots.* Santa Barbara, CA: ABC-CLIO, LLC.

National Center for Education Statistics, U.S. Department of Education. (2007). Schools and staffing survey. Retrieved from https://nces.ed.gov/surveys/sass/tables/sass0708_029_t12n.asp

National Center for Education Statistics, U.S. Department of Education. (2016). Trends in dropout and completion rates in the United States: Indicator 3 status dropout rate. Retrieved from https://nces.ed.gov/programs/dropout/ind_03.asp

National Center for Education Statistics, U.S. Department of Education. (2017). Status and trends in the education of racial and ethnic groups: Indicator 6 elementary and secondary enrollment. Retrieved from https://nces.ed.gov/programs/raceindicators/indicator_rbb.asp

Payne, K. (1994). *Influences on parental choice of children's early educational experiences.* (Unpublished doctoral dissertation). Michigan State University, East Lansing, MI.

Pew Research Center. (2015). *A majority of English-speaking Hispanics in the U.S. are bilingual.* Retrieved from http://www.pewresearch.org/fact-tank/2015/03/24/a-majority-of-english-speaking-hispanics-in-the-u-s-are-bilingual/

Pew Research Center. (2016). *Roughly half of Hispanics have experienced discrimination*. Retrieved from http://www.pewresearch.org/fact-tank/2016/06/29/roughly-half-of-hispanics-have-experienced-discrimination/

Reardon, S., & Galindo, C. (2003). *Hispanic children and the initial transition to schooling: Evidence from the early childhood longitudinal study*. Presentation to the National Academies/National Research Council, Panel on Hispanics in the United States.

Schneider, B., Martinez, S., & Owens, A. (2006). Barriers to educational opportunities for Hispanics in the U.S. In M. Tienda (Ed.), *Hispanics and the future of America*. Washington, DC: National Academies Press.

U.S. Census Bureau. (2016). Hispanic Heritage Month 2016. Retrieved from https://www.census.gov/newsroom/facts-for-features/2016/cb16-ff16.html

U.S. Census Bureau. (2018). Hispanic Heritage Month 2018. Retrieved from https://www.census.gov/newsroom/facts-for-features/2018/hispanic-heritage-month.html

Valenzuela, A. (1999). *Subtractive schooling: U.S. Mexican youth and the politics of caring*. Albany, NY: State University of New York Press.

Yosso, T. J. (2006). Whose culture has capital? A critical race theory discussion of community cultural wealth. In A. Dixson, C. Rousseau, & J. K. Donnor (Eds.), *Critical race theory in education: All God's children got a song* (pp. 113–136). New York, NY: Routledge.

· 2 ·

WHAT IS PARENTAL ENGAGEMENT?

I have chosen to examine Latinx parental engagement in part due to my membership in the Latinx social identity group and also because of the statistics regarding the Latinx population, educational outcomes, and the implications of those outcomes. According to the United States Census, Latinxs will become the nation's largest ethnic majority by the year 2060, or sooner. In 2017, 23 % of babies born in the United States were Latinx, for a total of 898,764 children (Center for Disease Control & Prevention, 2018). As described in chapter one, the 2016 U.S. Census data show the booming Latinx population matches the increasing number of Latinx students enrolled in kindergarten to grade 12. Despite the burgeoning number of the Latinx population and Latinx students in schools, American public-school systems are ill-equipped to educate this diversity of students.

Latinx students lag behind their Black, Asian, and White peers when it comes to high school graduation rates. Analyses pertaining to graduation rates for Latinx students compared to white students show that Latinx student high school graduation rates are still lower than their white counterparts (NCES, 2017).

The system of oppression holds Latinxs accountable for their dire statistics concerning education and other social issues they face. In so doing, the system of oppression excuses itself by blaming the victim, refusing to question the circumstances it [the system] creates which oppress Latinxs. Simultaneously, while Latinxs are being viewed as "deficient," the assets we bring to common areas, like education, are overlooked. There is robust literature on how Latinx students give their parents, caregivers, and community credit for their academic success. What I strive to do in this book is to examine Latinx parental engagement and how that engagement is utilized when students go to college. One of the strongest assets that Latinx students pack in their backpacks or suitcases when they head off to college are the lessons that they learned from their parents, caregivers, and community about who they are and where they come from. In order to understand the impact Latinx parents have on the long-term academic and occupational trajectories of their students, we have to understand Latinx parenting and the origins of the concept of parental engagement itself.

Understanding Parental Engagement

I started my education in the late 70s at the Holy Rosary School, a Catholic school in Jersey City, New Jersey. The school's population was predominantly white, with families having attended the school for almost a century, and students were primarily first-generation Italian-American. Students came from a "traditional" family that consisted of married heterosexual parents who bore children who attended the school. Monetary collections were taken at the affiliated Church on Sundays, and attendance to determine who went to church and offered a donation, was taken in the school on Mondays. To offset the cost of tuition, parents had the option of volunteering to work at the weekly Bingo nights held by the parish. My Mother, being a single parent and in need of subsidized tuition, worked at the Bingo hall on nights she wasn't scheduled to work at her paid position. As this was something she participated in so that we could continue attending that school, this was not viewed as parental engagement.

I recall other mothers acting as "class mothers" who would sometimes volunteer in the classroom, initiate the inclement weather "phone tree" and help serve lunch. This kind of participation was not an option for my Mother as her two—sometimes three—jobs would not permit it. My sister and I performed at many school plays, Christmas pageants and other events with no one in our audience, not because of a lack of caring on the part of my Mother, but due to the fact that her attendance at our performances took a back seat to the need to keep the lights on at home and to keep us in our school desks at Holy Rosary School. She did prioritize attending parent/teacher conferences because that is where she could hear how her investment in our education was paying off. Additionally, any feedback she received from the teacher during those conferences, also provided her with supplementary information she could use to continue to support the classroom teacher. If my teacher said I needed improvement in math, then Mom would prioritize my completion of math homework. Her participation at parent/teacher conferences was less daunting than her review of my report cards. She always returned home from parent/teacher conferences satisfied, having heard that we were diligent students, respectful, and smart. On one occasion that she would recall until the day she died, one of the nuns said, "your girls are so clean, they shine like new pennies." My Mother took great pride in the fact that cleanliness (something she instilled in us early and frequently) was part of our academic reputation. I can't imagine my reaction if someone were to claim that my Mother was not involved in my education due to her failure to attend Parent Teacher Association (PTA) meetings.

From my vantage point, she was constantly buzzing about education. Our book covers had to be *immaculate*. In August of every year, while I could hear my cousins playing outside and my extended family enjoying the barbecue, my sister and I were bathed and in bed by 7:30 pm while the sun was still out because my Mother was training us for an early bedtime for school. During the school year, breakfast was not optional because she always maintained that we needed full bellies for our brains to work in school. She once heard that cod liver oil "makes you smarter," and I vividly remember shutting my eyes tightly as she came at me with a spoonful of the putrid white liquid. Yet, her participation in teacher/parent conferences and her behind-the-scenes involvement in our education was not viewed as parental engagement. If her parenting style wasn't viewed as engaged, what then, did it mean to be an "engaged parent," and who was able to be seen as "engaged"? Further, where did the notion of engaged parenting even come from?

Origins of "Parental Involvement"

The term "parental involvement" was more widely used than "parental engagement." To be involved is to participate in, and to be engaged signifies meaningful contact or connection. For the purpose of this book, I have decided to use "parental engagement" because the narratives illustrated here demonstrate nothing short of committed, meaningful and connected engagement. Wherever the term "parental involvement" is used in this chapter, it is either the language used by specific researchers and reports or it is in reference to how the term parental involvement was being discussed and utilized. No matter the terminology, a parent's engagement and how it is viewed and valued by a school system has implications for the student and their families. Important in the understanding of parental engagement is how the concept originated.

According to Harro's (2008) "Cycle of Socialization," human beings are born, as scholars such as John Locke would agree, as "blank slates." It is not until we interact with those who are initially responsible for our overall well-being that the "slate" begins to take shape and we are socialized to live and operate within the world that surrounds us. Notice when a small child takes a tumble, they look up at their parents. I have noticed, unless a child is seriously hurt, that they gauge the level of their injury based on the reactions of their parents. I have seen with my own child and in observing other children, that if the parents look startled, the child cries. If the parents remain calm and reassure the child that they are okay, the child gets up and continues on. Anna, my daughter, now jumps up and declares "I'm okay!" after taking a spill. In this case, parents are our first teachers. They are not only responsible for our physical safety and nurturance, but they are also entrusted with the very earliest phases of our education, and in this respect, they teach us to have early interactions with the world around us. This view of the parent as having a critical impact on their children was echoed in the writings of theorists like Rosseau, Pestalozzi, and Froebel. It was Pestalozzi, who in 1951, wrote that the mother is, "the first to nourish her child's body, so should she, by God's order, be the first to nourish his mind" (Berger, 1991, p. 26).

Given the influence parents had over the education of their children, three theories emerged in the United States that spoke to parental involvement. They were theories that were influenced by European views on education and child rearing and the inherent nature of children. The first theory addressed the Calvinist belief that children were willful, and that willfulness was influenced by an evil from within. Breaking children of this "infant depravity" required that parents used discipline and that children needed to be broken from their willfulness (Berger, 1991, p. 211). The second theory was informed by the beliefs and writings of the likes of Rosseau, Pestalozzi, and Froebel, that supported the viewpoint that children were inherently good. Rosseau's work had influenced Pestalozzi's and this further informed Pestalozzi's student, Froebel. Frobel, like his teacher before him, held a particular belief in the influence on the mother and wrote, "Thus maternal instinct and love gradually introduce the child to his little outside world, proceeding from the whole to the part, from the near, to the remote" (Froebel cited in Berger, 1991, p. 211). Froebel believed in the goodness of children and the importance that care derived from the family played. In U.S. education, the period from 1870–1890 brought with it an increase in kindergartens and an increase in parental involvement in education, and parental education.

> It was Froebel's kindergartens that would be brought to the United States by a "prominent German immigrant, Margarethe Schurz, and by Elizabeth Peabody and Henry Barnard. Barnard, secretary of the Connecticut Board of Education, and later, U.S. commissioner of education, and Peabody, a kindergarten advocate and a sister-in-law of Horace Mann, promoted the Froebelian kindergarten movement throughout the United States." (p. 211)

The third theory was influenced by John Locke who believed that children were influenced by their environments, and he believed since children were influenced by their environment, intervention was therefore necessary (p. 212).

While the interests in kindergarten, childhood, and parental education programs were driven mainly from middle-class parents who were in line with the Rosseau, Pestalozzi and Froebelian views that children are inherently good; these programs were also a tool used for assimilation by "acculturating lower-class immigrant families into the mainstream culture" (p. 212). When immigrants arrived in the United States during the 1800s, kindergartens and programs like them were designed to ease the hardships of new Americans, to teach the newcomers of the "dominant culture's ways," and to indoctrinate immigrant parents with Americanized "moral and child rearing beliefs" (p. 212).

In the late 1800s, children's education and parental education programs saw the emergence of organizations dedicated to the study and support of both children and parents in education. They were: The Child Study Association of America in 1888, which "committed itself solely to the study of children and the spreading of good parenting practices" (p. 212); the Congress of Parents and Teachers in 1897, now recognized as the PTA; and the National Association of Colored Women in 1897. By 1897, almost 100 years after the new immigrants arrived in the United States, there were over 400 Free Kindergarten Association Programs in the U.S. (p. 212).

It was not long before the explosion of growth of these educational pro-grams would be noticed by other professional organizations, researchers, pub-lic schools, and the U.S. government. With the national and governmental attention, the interest in children and children's education was met with rap-id legislation and action. In 1909, the federal government held the first White House conference on the Care of Dependent Children; in 1912, the Chil-dren's Bureau was created; in 1914, the government published *Infant Care*. *Infant Care* was a pamphlet created to address the infant mortality rates. With mothers as its intended audience, from 1914 to its last issue in 1989 when it became *Bright Futures* the pamphlet provided information on everything from "cradle cap" to how to pass on cultural traditions. Also in 1914, the govern-ment passed the Smith-Lever Act, which provided 2,000 agents to inform individuals about home economics, agriculture and more; in 1917, they passed the Smith-Hughes Act, which supported child care and nutrition programs (Berger, 1991, p. 213).

By the 1920s, there were 26 major parent programs (p. 213). The de-creased number of immigrants being allowed into the U.S. also decreased the need to mainstream immigrants. The parent programs in place "were not es-tablished for new arrivals. They met the needs of middle-class parents who formed study groups for their own enlightenment, or, in some cases, there were developed in response to a need for health information about tubercu-losis or nutrition" (p. 213). In addition to the parental education program boom, the 1920s also saw a rapid increase of the numbers of parents in the PTA; new curricula for parental education groups; guides that covered men-tal health issues, nutrition, behavior, childhood development, discipline, and adolescent development (Berger, 1991); in 1925, the National Council of Parent Education; and the National Society for the Study of Education. As parent education became more professionalized, the roles of parents began to be defined as described by Zellman & Waterman (1988, p. 370):

> [T]he parents' role was dictated by the schools; ideally, parents would be helpers and supporters of what teachers and schools were doing. In particular, parents were encouraged to help with homework, join the PTA, provide merchandise for the bake sale and show up at times specified by the school, such as back to school night.

It is in the 1920s, with the professionalization of child and parent education programs and associations, that we see how parental involvement would be defined and manifested in schools.

Parental involvement wasn't merely professionalized, it was nationalized. With "buy in" from the national government, it seemed as U.S. support for children's and parental education was unstoppable. With its ability to decide which groups to include and which groups to omit, and its publication and dissemination of parenting guides to mothers, established by theorists as a child's first teacher, the government had the ability to shape what parenting looked like and defined what it was. The government now played a role in shaping how children would be raised and could tailor those practices. The paternalistic view of the government that they knew best how to rear children and could "teach" women and marginalized groups how to take care of their own babies is not new territory. The U.S. government has had a hand in the forced assimilation of Native Americans and African Americans, and the kidnapping of Native American children from their mothers to assimilate to U.S. culture (Rury, 2005). While funding was reduced to governmental programs with the stock market crash of 1929, parenting programs still received federal funding through the Great Depression of the 1930s and World War II of the 1940s. In 1954, although *Brown v. Board of Education, Topeka, KS* was upheld and presented an "opening" for statistical minorities, these marginalized parents would not have an opportunity to have an impact on child development and parental involvement until 1964. The Civil Rights Act of 1964 would grant equal rights—according to the law—to statistical racial minorities, and 1965 would introduce the Head Start Program. This program took the needs of parents into consideration and "empowered parents to make decisions" (Berger, 1991, p. 215). One of the most influential pieces of legislation passed in 1965 would be one that would reach far into the future of children and U.S. education. That Act was the Elementary and Secondary Education Act (ESEA) of 1965. The ESEA of 1965 was enacted on April 11, 1965 and originally authorized through 1970. It is reauthorized every five years, and the most recent iteration of the Act is what we know today as the "No Child Left Behind Act." In 2002, the No Child Left Behind Act (NCLB) reauthorized the ESEA, which authorizes funding for professional development, educational materials, funding for educational programs and initiatives such as programs that encourage parental involvement. In the NCLB Act, as with the ESEA, parental involvement is a required component that affects various state and federal education programs. In 2004, the Department of Education (DOE) produced a document from the NCLB defining parameters for educational funding titled: "Parental Involvement: Title I, Part A." In this document, the

DOE incorporated the National Parent Teacher Association's (PTA) definition to define parental involvement on a federal level as:

A-1. What is parental involvement under No Child Left Behind?

Parental involvement always has been a centerpiece of Title I. However, for the first time in the history of the ESEA, it has a specific statutory definition. The statute defines parental involvement as the participation of parents in regular, two-way, and meaningful communication involving student academic learning and other school activities, including ensuring—that parents play an integral role in assisting their child's learning; that parents are encouraged to be actively involved in their child's education at school; that parents are full partners in their child's education and are included, as appropriate, in decision-making and on advisory committees to assist in the education of their child; and that other activities are carried out, such as those described in section 1118 of the ESEA (Parental Involvement). [Section 9101(32), ESEA.]

According to this document:

[T]he new Title I, Part A is designed not only to help close the achievement gap between disadvantaged and minority students and their peers, but also to change the culture of America's schools so that success is defined in terms of student achievement and schools invest in every child. As indicated by the parental involvement provisions in Title I, Part A, the involvement of parents in their children's education and schools is critical to that process.

Under section A-1, parental involvement activities are further expounded and defined in section A-7 as:

A-7. What are the parental involvement provisions in section 1118 of the ESEA?

Title I, Part A provides for substantive parental involvement at every level of the program, such as in the development and implementation of the State and local plan, and in carrying out the LEA and school improvement provisions. Section 1118 contains the primary Title I, Part A requirements for SEAs, LEAs, and schools related to involving parents in their children's education. It is this section that identifies critical points in the process of improving teaching and learning where parents and the community can intervene and assist in school improvement. Although section 1118 is extensive in scope and has many requirements for LEAs and schools, the intent is not to be burdensome. These provisions reflect good practice in engaging families in helping to educate their children, because students do better when parents are actively involved in the education process, both at home and at school.

How Is Parental Involvement Understood?

One of the criticisms of parental involvement is that there is no one, cohesive, definition for it. Complicating the issue further and as I have alluded to in this chapter, there is a lack of uniformity in the use of the terms parental involvement and parental engagement. Researchers Grolnick and Slowiaczek define parental involvement as "the degree to which a parent dedicates resources of time and energy to his or her child in a given developmental or educational domain" (cited in Kuperminc, Darnell, & Alvarez-Jimenez, 2008, p. 470). The common theme between this definition and the definition set forth by the Department of Education in the NCLB is that parental involvement is a demonstrated act performed by a parent that directs that a parent be present in the education of their children. The dedication of "resources and time" and "active involvement" can be subject to interpretation.

In 1996, Dr. Joyce L. Epstein of John Hopkins University developed a parental involvement model called the "Six Types of Parental Involvement" that attempted to address the allocation of "resources and time." This model introduced the challenges and expected results for each of the types and the framework was intended to assist teachers and school administrators in developing school and family partnerships. Epstein's model included sample practices that described the type of parental involvement in greater detail. The six types are parenting; communication; volunteering; learning at home; decision making; and collaborating with community. The intent behind parenting is that in this first type, parenting was viewed as the ways in which families could establish supportive home environments and the ways in which schools could support families. Schools could assist parents with furthering their own education; assist families with health and nutrition; and schools could arrange for home visits to support parents. In the second type, communication, Epstein described a level of communication that would be "two way" and take part from the home to the school and from the school to the home. To achieve this, schools would have to be aware of any language barriers that might prevent parents from effectively communicating with the schools. To this end, schools should make translators available for non-English speaking families. Communication, in this type, would extend beyond language. She also proposed that schools could keep a regular schedule of sending notices such as making phone calls and sending newsletters. Type three, volunteering, describes the ways in which schools could recruit the help and support of parents. To accomplish this, she suggests that parents are surveyed and assessed based on time, location and specific talents of parents at the school; and that schools make allowances (i.e., family rooms or parent centers) for families in need of resources that would allow them to care for their families *and* volunteer on-site at a school. In type four, "learning at home," Epstein suggests accentuating parental styles with the schools providing resources and information on how parents can help their children with homework and making decisions within their education. This would involve keeping parents informed of what their children would need to accomplish and master in school for each grade level. Families would participate in setting goals and start conversations about higher education, and they would receive resources and support on how to monitor homework and be informed of what the school's homework policies were. Related to the topic of decision making, type five, "decision making" would support parents by including parents in the decision-making process and by developing parents in their leadership and advisory roles. To achieve this, parents would be linked to family representatives, and they would voice concern regarding their children's education through advocates. Finally, type six, "collaborating with community," would call upon the community's resources to reinforce school programs as well as the types of support already taking place within the home (i.e., parenting practices and supporting student development). Communities would then provide information to parents on the kinds of support systems available to students within the local community. The community would also work to creatively link student skills, interest and talent to student learning.

Building upon Dr. Epstein's "Six Types," the National Parent Teacher Association (PTA)—the same organization whose definition of parental involvement was included in the NCLB—created the "National Standards for Family-School Partnerships" (National PTA, 2011) (Table 2.1). The implementation guide offers six goals and initiatives that address the ways in which schools and parents can work collaboratively to support students. Taking Epstein's work into account, the PTA Standards also consider what schools can do to anticipate obstacles that would stand in the way of parents being involved within the school.

Table 2.1: National standards for family-school partnerships.

Standard	Explanation of Standard
Standard 1: "Welcoming all families into the school community"	"Families are active participants in the life of the school, and feel welcomed, valued, and connected to each other, to school staff, and to what students are learning and doing in class."
Standard 2: "Communicating effectively"	"Families and school staff engage in regular, two-way, meaningful communication about student learning."
Standard 3: "Supporting student success"	"Families and school staff continuously collaborate to support students' learning and healthy development both at home and at school and have regular opportunities to strengthen their skills and knowledge to do so effectively."
Standard 4: "Speaking up for every child"	"Families are empowered to be advocates for their own and other children, to ensure that students are treated fairly and have access to learning opportunities that will support their success."
Standard 5: "Sharing power"	"Families and school staff are equal partners in decisions that affect parents and families and together inform, influence, and create policies, practices, and programs."
Standard 6: "Collaborating with community"	"Families and school staff collaborate with community members to connect students, families, and staff to expanded learning opportunities, community services, and civic participation."

Source: Author.

Epstein's "Six Types of Parental Involvement" and the National PTA's "National Standards for Family-School Partnerships" have their merit. What is missing, however, is the reality that schools are not welcoming places for all families in that racial bias, stereotypes, and teacher's perceptions need to be addressed as potential obstacles to these standards. Additionally, some of Epstein's suggestions fail to take into account conceivable racial and socio-economic stigmas families might experience. The work of Lareau (2011) supports the fact that not all families feel comfortable with teachers conducting home visits. There exist cultural misunderstandings between schools and homes. For example, if a teacher enters a home and sees it in disarray with clothes strewn on the furniture, toys cluttering the house and a pile of dishes in the sink, depending on their cultural perspective, they might view this home as unfit. However, if they look at this scene from an asset-based perspective, they might say that the clothes strewn on the furniture indicates the child has clothing, the toys indicate that the child has something with which to occupy themselves, and the pile of dishes in the sink indicates that the child has access to food. Before a teacher should enter any students home, they must first be aware of their own biases and how their own lived experiences and expectations can influence how they view a student's home life. Similar issues exist in the Epstein's area on communication. A translator hired by the school to communicate with parents must be willing to offer complete and accurate translations. Majo Correa, a Mount Holyoke College alumna, noticed that translators in the public school she was affiliated with were not offering accurate translations during Individualized Education Plans (IEPs) with Spanish-speaking parents. They would not translate all of what was being said from English, and their messages were not being appropriately translated from Spanish. In this case, there was really no way for a Spanish-speaking parent to be a full participant in the academic lives of their child because they were only receiving 50% of the information. To address this problem, Majo created "Spanish Corps" so Spanish-speaking families could be assisted in being fully informed of the status of their children. The idea that parents can volunteer on-site at a school neglects to address myriad hurdles parents might face. If, however, volunteering took into account the cultural capital that Latinx parents offer, then social capital could be utilized to help parents volunteer at the school in an off-site capacity as parents could support the school on their own now-school hours schedule and use the social networking they had access to. Epstein's "learning at home" speaks directly to ways that Latinx parents demonstrate engagement in homework completion, and in actively supporting the work and policies of the classroom teacher. While not all parents would be prepared to start conversations on higher education, schools and guidance counselors could work with families on learning the vocabulary of higher education to make those conversations possible and equitable among all families. Her fifth recommendation on utilizing community is hugely effective and welcomed in Latinx communities, further details of which I will be addressing in chapter four.

The "National Standards for Family-School Partnerships" standards are lofty at best, and while commendable, do not address the potential issues of bias that may be held by teachers and school administrators. Yes, families should absolutely feel welcomed, valued, and connected. However, how are parents made to feel welcomed, and how can the lives of those families be celebrated in culturally appropriate and respectful ways? When it comes to celebrating diversity, schools seem to subscribe to the curriculum relevant to monthly heritage months, further simultaneously tokenizing and marginalizing students of color. I once walked into a charter school in Western Massachusetts for a job interview. As soon as I entered the foyer, I could feel my jaw drop at the sight of at least twenty different world flags. The principal, seeing the stunned look on my face, anticipated my question and said, "each flag represents the different nations our students come from." As I hurried to catch up with her as she walked down the hall, I asked "but what if you get a new student?" Without missing a beat, she shrugged and replied, "then we get another flag." Welcoming families starts at the front door, and the first person a parent meets can make an incredible first impression. So too, does the décor, bulletin boards, and how families can see themselves reflected back in the life of the school. The communication standard introduces a similar problem to Epstein's communication standard. If teachers and school administrators don't value the participation of parents, and parents feel that they are unwelcomed in the school, healthy communication between the two is a near-impossibility. Schools and parents can and should work collaboratively on supporting student success, however, Latinx parental engagement contributions need to be seen and valued as part of that meaningful contribution. Sharing power equally is only effective if both parties—parents and teachers—are seen as equals. When Latinx parents are already dismissed as "those" parents before meeting the teacher, there is no shared equality.

Importance of Parental Engagement

Why is there such an emphasis on parental support and engagement? One explanation may be the research that demonstrates a correlation between parental engagement in education and academic achievement. Research indicates that families have a strong impact on the educational performance of their children (Coleman, 1975; Epstein, Croates, Salinas, Sanders, & Simon, 1997; Finn, 1998; Kellaghan, Sloane, Alvarez, & Bloom, 1993; Sheldon, 2005). Research further shows a connection between parental engagement in schools and the attendance rates, academic achievement, attitudes, and record of continued education (Henderson & Berla, 1994; Hickman, 1995). Evidence also demonstrates a direct link between parental engagement and student academic achievement (Ascher, 1988; Baker & Soden, 1998; Chavkin, 1993; Chavkin & Gonzalez, 1995; Epstein, 1996; Floyd, 1998; Petersen, 1989). These findings are also supported by Inger's (1992) assertion that "there is considerable evidence that parent involvement leads to improved student achievement, better school attendance, and reduced dropout rates, and that these improvements occur regardless of the economic, racial, or cultural background of the family" (p. 1).

Interpretations of Parental Engagement: Parents and Educational Institutions

The literature on parental engagement asserts that there is an association between parental engagement in education and the academic outcomes of their children, but how is this engagement manifested? As stated earlier in this chapter, the expectations regarding parental engagement in education was originally defined and prescribed by educational professionals in the 1920s. In order for parents to be "involved" (by school expectations) they had to take on the role of the "helper" and supporter of what the school asked them to support and help with, and they were to "show up" to school events when the school asked them to (Berger, 1991). These descriptions of parental engagement have not changed much since the 1920s. Almost 80 years later, in 1996, the DOE's Office of Educational Research and Improvement released statistics on parental engagement in school related activities. Similar to what I experienced in my own education, the characteristics defining parental engagement in the report were: attendance at general meetings; attendance at scheduled meetings with a teacher; attendance at a school event; volunteerism or committee service; and homework help (Child Trends Data Bank, 2003). Teachers, who are informed and held to national educational standards, support the definition, understanding, and standard manifestation of parental engagement. In interviews with teachers, Scribner, Young, and Pedroza (1999) found that teachers defined parent involvement as attendance (including formal meetings and events) and volunteerism (providing assistance at the school). Of note is that while the DOE, PTA, NCLB, administrations, and teachers have one perception of parental engagement, some parents have a different understanding altogether.

One explanation for the inconsistency between the understanding of parental engagement among teachers and parents is the fact that parental engagement is difficult to define. In this sense, it can be said that parental engagement lies in the eye of the beholder. Parental engagement and how it is experienced and manifested differs, and these differences are culturally based (Trumbull, Rothstein-Fisch, Greenfield, & Quiroz, 2001). Supporting this notion, Ascher (1988), states:

> Parent involvement may easily mean quite different things to people. It can mean advocacy: parents sitting on councils and committees, participating in the decisions and operation of schools. It can mean parents serving as classroom aides, accompanying a class on an outing, or assisting teachers in a variety of other ways, either as volunteers or for wages. It can also conjure up images of teachers sending notes home to parents, or of parents working on bake sales and other projects that bring schools much needed support. Increasingly, parent involvement means parents initiating learning activities at home to improve their children's performance in school: reading to them, helping them with homework, playing educational games, discussing current events and so on (p. 109)

If schools and parents hold differing views on parental involvement, so too may they hold different targets regarding manifestations of involvement (Trumbull et al., 2001). One group of parents who have consistently received criticism for a perceived lack of involvement, and whose understanding of parental involvement differs from the ED standard, is Latinx parents. Arguably, the same can be said of African American, Native American, Asian American, and immigrant parents coming to the United States from all reaches of the world, which is that their perceptions of parental involvement also differ from the historical standard.

References

Ascher, C. (1988). Improving the school-home connection for poor and minority urban students. *Urban Review, 20*(2), 109–123.

Baker, A. J., & Soden, L. M. (1998). *The challenges of parent involvement research.* New York, NY: ERIC Clearinghouse on Urban Education.

Berger, E. H. (1991). Parent involvement: Yesterday and today. *The Elementary School Journal, 91*(3), 209–219.

Centers for Disease Control and Prevention. (November 7, 2018). National Vital Statistics Reports (NVSR), Vol. 67, No. 8: Births: Final Data for 2017. Retrieved from https://www.kff.org/other/state-indicator/births-by raceethnicity/?currentTimeframe=0&selectedDistributions=hispanic--total&selectedRows=%7B%22wrapups%22:%7B%22united-states%22:%7B%7D%7D%7D&sortModel=%7B%22colId%22:%22Location%22,%22sort%22:%22asc%22%7D

Chavkin, N. F. (1993). *Families and schools in a pluralistic society.* New York, NY: State University of New York Press.

Chavkin, N. F., & Gonzalez, D. L. (1995). *Forging partnerships between Mexican American parents and the schools.* Charleston, WV: ERIC Clearinghouse on Rural Education and Small Schools. (ERIC Document Reproduction Service No. ED382412).

Child Trends Data Bank. (2003). *Parent involvement in schools.* http://www.childtrendsdatabank.org/pdf/39_PDF.pdf

Coleman, J. S. (1975). Comments on schools. *Today's Education, 64,* 27–29.

Epstein, J. L. (1996). Perspectives and previews in research and policy for school, family, and community partnerships. In A. Booth & J. F. Dunn (Eds.), *Family-school links* (pp. 209–246). Mahwah, NJ: Erlbaum.

Epstein, J. L., Croates, L., Salinas, K. C., Sanders, M. G., & Simon, B. S. (1997). *School, family, and community partnerships: Your handbook in action.* Thousand Oaks, CA: Corwin Press.

Finn, J. D. (1998). *Class size and students at risk: What is known? What is next?* National Institute on the Education of At-risk Students. Office of Educational Research and Improvement (OERI). Washington, D.C.: United States Department of Education.

Floyd, L. (1998). Joining hands: A parental involvement program. *Urban Education, 33*(1), 123–135.

Hagan, J. F., Shaw, J. S., & Duncan, P. M. (Eds.). (2008). *Bright futures: Guidelines for health supervision of infants, children and adolescents.* (3rd ed.). Elk Grove Village, IL: American Academy of Pediatrics.

Harro, B. (2008). Updated version of "The cycle of socialization" (2000). In M. Adams, W. J. Blumenfeld, R. Castañeda, H. W. Hackman, M. L. Peters, & X. Zúñiga (Eds.), *Readings for diversity and social justice* (pp. 463–469). New York, NY: Routledge.

Henderson, A. T., & Berla, N. (Eds.). (1994). *A new generation of evidence: The family is critical to student achievement.* Washington, D.C.: National Committee for Citizens in Education.

Hickman, C. W. (1995). *The future of high school success: The importance of parent involvement programs.* Retrieved from http://horizon.unc.edu/projects/HSJ/Hickman.html

Inger, M. (1992). *Increasing the school involvement of Hispanic parents.* ERIC Clearinghouse on Urban Education. (ERIC Document Reproduction Service No. EDO-UD-92-3).

Kellaghan, T., Sloane, K., Alvarez, B., & Bloom, B. S. (1993). *The home environment and school learning: Promoting parental involvement in the education of children.* San Francisco, CA: Jossey Bass.

Kuperminc, G. P., Darnell, A. J., & Alvarez-Jimenez, A. (2008). Parent involvement in the academic adjustment of Latino middle and high school youth: Teacher expectations and school belonging as mediators. *Journal of Adolescence, 31*(4), 469–483.

Lareau, A. (2011). *Unequal childhoods: Class, race, and family life.* (2nd ed.). Berkeley, CA: University of California Press.

National PTA. (2011). National Standards for Family-School Partnerships. Retrieved from https://www.pta.org/home/run-your-pta/National-Standards-for-Family-School-Partnerships

No Child Left Behind Act. (2002). Pub. L. No. 107–110, 115 Stat. 1425. 20 USCA §§6301 et seq.

Peterson, D. (1989). *Parent involvement in the educational process.* Eugene, OR: ERIC Clearinghouse on Educational Management. (ERIC Document Reproduction Service No. ED312776).

Rury, J. (2005). *Education and social changes: Themes in the history of American schooling.* Hillsdale, NJ: Erlbaum.

Scribner, J. D., Young, M. D., & Pedroza, A. (1999). Building collaborative relationships with parents. In P. Reyes, J. D. Scribner, & A. P. Scribner (Eds.), *Lessons from high-performing Hispanic schools: Creating learning communities* (pp. 36–60). New York, NY: Teachers College Press.

Sheldon, S. B. (2005). Testing a structural equations model of a partnership program implementation and involvement. *The Elementary School Journal, 106,* 171–187.

Trumbull, E., Rothstein-Fisch, C., Greenfield, P. M., & Quiroz, B. (2001). *Bridging cultures between home and schools: A guide for teachers.* Mahwah, NJ: Erlbaum.

U.S. Census Bureau. (2016). Hispanic Heritage Month 2016. Retrieved from https://www.census.gov/newsroom/facts-for-features/2016/cb16-ff16.html

U.S. Census Bureau. (2018). Hispanic Heritage Month 2018. Retrieved from https://www.census.gov/newsroom/facts-for-features/2018/hispanic-heritage-month.html

United States Department of Labor. (1935). *Infant Care.* Children's Bureau Publication No. 8. Washington, DC: U.S. Government Printing Office.

Zellman, G. L., & Waterman, J. M. (1998). Understanding the impact of parent school involvement on children's educational outcomes. *Journal of Educational Research, 91*(6), 370–380.

· 3 ·

UNDERSTANDING LATINX
PARENTAL ENGAGEMENT

There are many reasons that can explain the academic underachievement of Latinx students. Some of these reasons may include conditions of poverty resulting in lack of access to resources, language and communication barriers, low parental educational attainment, and low teacher expectations. Another reason may be the relationship between parents and schools (Scribner, 1999). Given the dire statistics on Latinx academic underperformance and the research that evidences parental involvement as a factor in academic achievement (Antrop-Gonzalez, Velez, & Garrett, 2005; Ascher, 1988; Chavkin, 1993; Chavkin & Gonzalez, 1995; Epstein, 1996; Floyd, 1998; Peterson, 1989), it is imperative that schools and Latinx parents have a common understanding of parental engagement so that together, they can work toward comparable and attainable goals.

I was raised in a working-class home with a single parent whose annual income was $25,000. We lived in the house that my Mother purchased by saving the purchase price of $6,000. Our home was in an economically depressed area where residents were predominantly African American and it abutted a truck yard, the last stop on our dead-end street. Other homes on my street had a backyard, but we had a front yard which meant that when the cold wind blew, we did not enjoy the shelter of neighboring homes. The downstairs floors were covered with linoleum, but the centennial house had concrete floors, and no insulation. There was no central cooling or heating system. The first person to rise in the morning was the person who needed to turn the oven on and open the oven door to heat the first floor so we could have breakfast. When we came home from school in the wintertime, we were instructed to change into our footed pajamas and complete our homework upstairs because the first floor was unbearably cold. Before we went to bed, my Mother gave us each a shot glass full of anisette to keep us warm while we slept. My hair at the time was at least two-feet-long, and as it was too long to wash and dry in the morning, I had to wash my hair at night in a bucket used for hair washing as there was a separate bucket for washing our bodies. We kept a cat, and not because we wanted one, but because we needed something to hunt the rats that threatened to gnaw their way through the ceiling tiles above our bed. They wanted to be warm, too.

During the time that my father lived in the home with us, he was known to spend all of his weekly earnings to support his alcoholism. I remember several instances where his unwillingness to help pay for utilities resulted in our family of six using a Coleman cooler to preserve our groceries as the electricity was cut off. Mom still made us do our homework, but we did it by the light of a camping lantern. No one at our school knew what we were going through, and as we were star students, no one had cause to worry. There did exist somewhat of a communication barrier as my Mother did not have a formal education and she was single-handedly trying to navigate all of us through our education. Sometimes she asked me to help decipher the meanings of words in teachers notes, but I was rather unhelpful that I was just a child, myself.

I bring these experiences up because poverty resulting in lack of access to resources, language and communication barriers and low parental educational attainment *can* be reasons for academic underachievement, but in the case of my Mother's method of parental engagement, she was determined to make do with what she had. However, a Latinx student can have access to resources, live with fluent, college educated English-speaking parents and still experience academic failure. Again, I do not claim that Latinxs lead cookie-cutter lives with cookie-cutter resolutions. This is an attempt to shed light on a dark corner of parental engagement.

Interpretation of Parental Engagement: Latinx Parents

As it has been established through the historical accounts of parental involvement in U.S. education, schools and teachers have, for almost a century, asked parents to assimilate into the mainstream culture. Now, in 2018, when schools have a drastically different demographic than recorded in 1920, it is time to attend to not merely attract—but support—the diversity within U.S. schools. One of the ways to support the changing demographics and the largest growing population of Latinx students is to better understand the ways in which Latinx parents view, interpret, and manifest parental engagement as well as the cultural explanations for the reasons that these views are held.

To better understand Latinx parental engagement, teachers need to understand one main idea: that for Latinx parents, education is of the utmost importance and Latinx parents demonstrate the value of education through cultural practices. These practices include voicing their regard for education; holding a cultural understanding of education; transmitting the cultural value of education through narratives; and demonstrating the importance of education through imparting behaviors and habits to their children.

My Mother had a mantra when it came to her role as a parent and my classroom teacher's role. "I'm the boss in this house, and she's the boss in that class. You respect her like you would respect me." Those rules were crystal clear any time a teacher or school official tried in any way to meddle with her parenting. If my Mom wasn't going to tell the teacher how to teach, then it was in the teacher's best interest not to interfere with her parenting.

Throughout the literature, Latinx parents voiced and demonstrated that culturally, there are clear boundaries as to the role of the school and the role of the parent. The school's primary responsibility is to foster and instill knowledge (Carger, 1997; Chavkin, 1991; Chavkin & Gonzalez, 1995; Trumbull, Rothstein-Fisch, Greenfield, & Quiroz, 2001) and the role of the parents is to care for their children and to teach them values, respect, and good behavior (Carger, 1997; Chavkin & Gonzalez, 1995; Espinosa, 1995; Trumbull et al., 2001). When parents are asked to perform duties and be engaged in their children's education in ways that interfere with their cultural understanding of engagement, they are unclear on what their roles are (Sosa, 1997). What the schools describe as engagement may be read as interference by Latinx parents. Since educators are highly valued and respected in the Latinx culture (Chavkin & Gonzalez, 1995), this type of interference is viewed by Latinx parents to be highly disrespectful (Chavkin, 1991; Chavkin & Gonzalez, 1995; Espinosa, 1995; Trumbull et al., 2001).

If parental engagement is viewed and valued differently than the view of schools, what does Latinx parental engagement mean, and how is it manifested at home and at school? In order to understand how Latinx parents view parental engagement in the education of their children, it is first important to establish how Latinxs view education.

Latinx Parental Regard for Education

My abuela lived in Caguas, Puerto Rico before she permanently moved to the mainland in 2003. Caguas is in a mountainous region of Puerto Rico and her tin-roofed house was remote, but also had a wraparound porch and birds eye view of the Puerto Rican mountains. Abuela was popular in her neighborhood, and Sundays were busy at her home with visitors to spend time with "Doña Maria." We would visit abuela ever summer, and I clearly remember the day she had a special visitor. My Mom interrupted my play with the local children to lead me by the hand to stand in front of a well-dressed woman with long black hair. Mom said "Jennifer, this woman is a *teacher*." She might as well have said astronaut, brain surgeon, or President of the United States with the way in which my Mom showed her reverence for teachers. My Mother's introduction to this visitor was something that I will always remember because it showed me how my Mom felt about education.

The dismal statistics regarding Latinxs in the United States portray Latinx students as not being as invested in their education as their peers. Statistics on low-academic achievement for Latinx students implicate parents because, as indicated earlier, parents are our first teachers, and parental engagement is a factor in academic achievement. The logic would presume that if students are underperforming in schools, it is at the fault of the parents who serve as our first educators. Many school teachers maintain these negative assumptions of Latinx parents as apathetic, uncaring and uninvolved in regard to the education of their children. These negative viewpoints impact the interaction between teachers and parents in condescending ways (Ceballo, 2004). It is these negative beliefs and biases that need to be addressed before schoolteachers and administrators can claim adopting policies that claim to be racially inclusive. A more careful and clear understanding of the value placed on education by Latinxs can lead to more positive interactions and as a by-product, more positive outcomes.

In contrast to the belief that Latinx parents do not hold a high regard for education, the literature on the topic of Latinx parental engagement shows that Latinx parents hold and communicate high expectations for their children and express a desire to participate in their academic success (Delgado-Gaitán, 1994; Moles et al., 1993; Trueba & Delgado-Gaitán, 1988). Data from the Child Trends Data Bank (2018) indicates that, like my Mother, Latinx parents prioritize parent/teacher conferences and general meetings but don't have high rates of attendance in other areas. When compared to whites, the data on engagement is as follows:

Table 3.1: Latinx parental engagement by event.

	General Meetings	Parent/Teacher Conferences	School/Class Event	Volunteerism or Committee Service
White parents	89%	79%	86%	43%
Latinx parents	87%	75%	71%	36%

Source: Child Trends Dara Bank (2018).

Although the belief in the power of education is conveyed differently by Latinxs than it is by whites, a significant number of studies specify that Latinxs in fact hold a firm belief in the value of education and transmit that value to their children (Arellano & Padilla, 1996; Okagaki & Frensch, 1998). Further findings uphold the idea that Latinx families hold high aspirations for the academic success of their children (Delgado-Gaitán, 1994; Moll et al., 1993). Parental demonstration of the value of an education has a significantly positive impact on their children. In cases of high-achieving Latinx students, Latinx parental involvement is cited as a factor attributed to academic success, and a consistent factor for positive educational outcomes is the significance that the Latinx family plays in the lives of students (Antrop-González et al., 2005; Ceballo, 2004; Rivera, 1997; Valencia & Black, 2007; Waterman, 2008). Parents are also highly influential in regard to occupational aspirations. A study by Behnke, Piercy, and Diversi (2004) shows a relationship between the aspirations of Latinx parents and those of their children. Results of the study indicated where Latinx parents stated that they wanted to further their education; their children expressed a similar aspiration. For example, if a father expressed wanting to be a mechanic, his child would express interest in engineering. The study further indicated that the reverse was true in that parents with little or no occupational and/or educational aspirations had children with similarly low or unnamed aspirations. Support for education, high expectations, and Latinx parents as a link between the realms of home life and school life are themes that are recurring in the literature. Setting and meeting high expectations (which includes the completion of school through graduation), influencing students through support and motivation (Zalaquett, 2006), the expression of the desire for children to further their education and to surpass the educational attainment of their parents, is also pervasive in the literature on Latinx parenting behaviors (Lara-Alecio, Irby, & Ebener, 1997; Valencia & Black, 2002). Latinx parents have power and influence in transmitting the value of education to their children, and that power is significant in regard to aspirational, educational, and occupational outcomes. Parents are aware of the fact that they, similar to the beliefs and expectations held in the 1920s, are "helpers" when it comes to the education of their children, but that type of assistance is manifested differently. Seeing themselves in this way also suggests that Latinx parents possess an understanding of their boundaries as "home" educators and teachers as "formal" educators. They see their roles as parents as a support to the role of the school teacher, and they see the values taught and reinforced at home as being supplemental to what is being taught within their children's classrooms. In doing so, Latinx parents view their contributions to the education of their children as well as their teacher's contributions as being "commitments of value" (Waterman, 2008, p. 154). One of the ways that Latinx parents transmit the value of education is to first establish what education means in a Latinx family.

Education as a Cultural Value

There is a difference in the meaning conveyed through the English word "education," and the Spanish understanding within the word "*educación*." The challenges presented by translation do not fully allow for a deep and accurate account of what the word *educación* means for the Latinx people. In Latinx culture, possessing or seeking to obtain an education means more than merely having formal educational training. Latinx parents who hold the cultural value of *educación* do not differentiate between formal education and moral training and see both as having equal importance in child rearing (Reese, Balzano, Gallimore, & Goldenberg, 1995). The academic and nonacademic aspects of *educación* hold a great deal of significance for Latinxs actively engaged in the education of their children (Halgunseth, Ispa, & Rudy, 2006). Not all Latinx families and students subscribe to this belief that education is comprised of both academic training and moral values because not all Latinxs come from the same countries of origin or level of acculturation. However, this concept provides insight into the academic experiences and realities of some Latinx students and their parents (Woolley, Kol, & Bowen, 2009).

For those parents who do subscribe to the concept of *educación* know that the framework of *educación* has powerful implications for the education of their children (Goldenberg & Gallimore, 1995; Mehan, Villanueva, Hubbard, & Lintz, 1996; Reese et al., 1995; Valdés, 1996). *Educación* deals with moral training and values that are taught by parents and it deals with the academic training that takes place in the classroom and is taught by the classroom teacher. Parents see their role as providing a foundation of morals and values necessary to experience positive educational outcomes. A student who is considered to be *bien educada/o* ("well-educated" and good-mannered) is a good person who demonstrates good behavior, who demonstrates respect (*respeto*) for those considered to be adults with authority (such as teachers), who is on the right "life-path" and who performs well academically (Reese et al., 1995). In terms of direct parenting and transmission of values, Latina mothers in particular concede that while they may lack formal educational training, they can enhance the educational experiences of their children by providing them with *una buena educación* (a good education). This is the way in which they can have a direct and positive impact on the education of their children (Waterman, 2008). The responsibility of providing children with a good education does not rest solely on the shoulders of Latinx parents but is a collaborative process that involves the extended family and the community (Espinoza-Herold, 2007). Families see personal character and social skills (Valdés, 1996; Villenas & Moreno, 2001) as influential factors in being "well educated" and play a role in helping their children to be "good people." Parents who put the concept of *educación* into practice see that they take on the role of motivators and encouragers (Azmitia, Cooper, Garcia, & Dunbar, 1996; Delgado-Gaitán, 1994; Valdés, 1996). When parents feel that they are limited in their abilities to assist students in the realm of formal schooling, they feel that their primary responsibility where the education of their children is concerned is to have discussion with them about good and appropriate behavior (Auerbach, 2006).

While I will not go into great detail regarding the class associations that accompany the notion of being *bien educada/o*, the translation suggests that there is a connection between being "cultured" and "classed." To be *bien edu-cado* is also in some instances, to aspire to a higher socioeconomic class. This is not a novel idea as the idea that education and culture are related goes as far back as Greek society and the teachings of Plato (Berger, 1991). Ancient cultures "imparted skills, mores, and values of the time, influenced by their life experiences, the environment in which they lived, and their culture" (p. 210).

Latinxs also impart the mores and values that shaped their lives and one such value related to the concept of is *respeto*, or respect. Essential to good and appropriate behavior and essential in being perceived as being *bien educado/a* is the concept of *respeto*. Explained by Halgunseth et al. (2006), *respeto* or "harmonious interpersonal relationships through respect for self and others' particularly elders, suggests that Latino students are raised to respect elders and the roles they serve, which includes adults in the family and with adults at school" (p. 286). I was thirty-four years old when my family traveled to Puerto Rico for a family vacation. We were on my cousin's veranda when I heard the sound of the Puerto Rican mascot, the tree frog known as the coquí. I was determined to find the tiny frog whose song I was familiar with, but who I'd never seen in person. My Mother was talking with my cousin when I spotted the small brown frog and I kept looking desperately back at my Mom who was still deep in conversation. I walked over to her several times but could not find a respectful way to interrupt. I would walk between my Mother's engaging gossip session and the coquí until the coquí decided to hop away. When I told my Mother that I had seen a *real, live coquí* she asked why I hadn't told her. "Because you told me never to interrupt when you were talking to a grown up." Respeto was so deeply ingrained in our upbringing that none of my Mother's children ever swore in front of her out of respect. In school settings, the relationships between parents, students and teachers are considered to be vital in the formal educational experiences of students. Within informal interactions, research documents that when school personnel (administrators and teachers) show respect for parents, parental engagement in school increases (De Gaetano, 2007). Such relationships and collaborations could lead to a "unified front" message where respect is a value upheld in the direct environments that influence student learning and student learning outcomes. In my short term as a high school teacher, I found that when students knew I had a mutually respectful relationship with their parents, student behavior changed in that it was almost as if they now had a parental presence in the classroom. Calling student homes was a common habit for me, and I made sure that the first phone call home was always a call with good news. I remember the first of these calls to a Latinx home. When I introduced myself as the teacher, the parent on the line immediately thought I was calling with a complaint. The mom asked me to hold while she got the student's father on the other line. I reintroduced myself and told both parents about the great job their child was doing in school and how proud I was of them. The student's mother asked me to hold again as she gathered extended family members to listen in. She summarized what I had said to them in Spanish and I could hear satisfied chattering on the other end. She thanked me for the call and told me to call back for any reason and that I had their support. I had their support, I firmly believe, because I showed respect to the family even though I am quite sure that my student's parents were my age. I was showing them respect for what they taught their child, I was showing respect and caring for their child, and I was treating them as equals, and more importantly, as experts on the person who sat in my class every day. Parents, specifically mothers, feel that it is important that they teach their children to be respectful of teachers (Waterman, 2008), and mothers who lack a formal education have a documented valued respect for authority figures in school settings and relay that value to their children (Harding, 2006).

Parenting Practices

Narrative Interventions

While *educación* and *respeto* are concepts that are conveyed passively, Latinx parents also utilize active parenting practices to demonstrate their commitment to the education of their children. These more active practices are demonstrated through communication and story-telling, monitoring, and moral support. The communication that education is important is demonstrated through the use of narrative teaching known as *consejos*, or advice and teachings used by Latinx adults to guide and nurture Latinx youth (Delgado-Gaitán, 1994). The work done by Villanueva (1996) establishes that consejos was the primary way in which less educated adults demonstrated a key form of Latinx parent support for education (Delgado-Gaitán, 1994; Gándara, 1995; Valdés, 1996; Villanueva, 1996). A Latinx parent might lack financial resources, but they have a legacy to share through the stories of their lived experiences.

Consejos are used to illustrate a lesson and these kinds of narrative interventions empower students with the confidence to take responsibility for their education (Delgado-Gaitán, 1994). Important to dispensing the wisdom held in *consejos*, cautionary tales similar to those employed through the emergent parenting styles are used as a means to redirect students from the parents' own example and choices, and they are used to motivate students to perform well in school (Gándara, 1995; Goldenberg & Gallimore, 1995; Stanton-Salazar, 2001; Treviño, 2004). The *consejos*, which are repeated and handed down in Spanish, are a form of cultural capital in which the primary knowledge base is culturally rooted. In the absence of formal education, parents rely on cultural frameworks like *consejos* to guide their children toward positive educational outcomes. The practice of sharing one's *consejos* that have been learned serves a dual purpose. First, it is a means by which Latina mothers can promote and support academic achievement. Second, it is the means by which Latinxs preserve their own culture and tradition that takes place within their families. An aspect of the cultural tradition being maintained is the acceptance of the validity held within *consejos*. It provides a structure in which a relationship of reciprocity can thrive. Adults dispense the wisdom of *consejos*, children follow the *consejos* because a pattern of validity and trust has been established and in turn, parents trust and support their children's ability to make sound academic decisions. Adults stress the importance of *consejos* through repeating them as in "*Quien no oye consejos, no llega a viejo*" (Someone who doesn't heed advice won't ever live long enough to get old), and youth are entrusted to exercise their free will in following or not following their advice (Espinoza-Herold, 2007). This demonstration of the utilization of consejos in Latinx families as guiding principles that reinforce values, hopes, and dreams (Delgado-Gaitán, 1994; Valdés, 1996), calls attention to the influence of culture and family in experiences of Latinx youth. In terms of motivation, *consejos* are used to bolster students with messages, such as "*¡Si se puede!*" (Yes, you can!) as well as advice on how to seek out opportunities instead of becoming discouraged when obstacles to achievement of any kind are presented.

Parents also give *consejos*, not only through the use of cultural proverbs but through their own life experiences. They convey the real-life hardships associated with the lack of a formal education and conveyed mixed feelings ranging from regret and anger regarding their own "missed opportunities" and lessons about life paths they chose in contrast to what they felt their children should do. This regret in not having completed a formal education is used as the basis for their commitment to prioritizing the value of an education for their children. Additionally, they view an education in the United States as an opportunity not to be wasted (Auerbach, 2006).

Where Latinx parents felt that they could not act as educational role models, they used their stories of life experience as cautionary tales to advise their children against repeating parental patterns. Additionally, some Latinx parents will use disgraced family members as examples of what not to be. I was often reminded that there were family members who never finished school, and as a result, led dismal lives.[1] Cautionary tales were accompanied by lessons regarding the importance of a strong work ethic. In the research conducted on migrant workers with successful children, Treviño noted that "parents were promoting their children's mental toughness as *luchistas* (proactive strivers) who could overcome obstacles" (cited in Auerbach, 2006, p. 282). Within the same theme, López (2001) described how migrant worker parents related and associated hard work in school to hard manual labor, and how these lessons were regarded by Latinx parents as an example of parental involvement. The idea of students needing to work as hard in school as parents work as hard in the fields is described in the works of Gándara (1995) and López (2001), where parents teach their children that diligent study and effort yields success (Reese et al., 1995) and where parents impress upon their children that it is the "job to study 100%" (Auerbach, 2006, p. 281). My critique of this parenting strategy is that it can create stress in Latinx student lives. One participant in my doctoral research study lamented that as hard as she worked, she could never catch up to her roommate, although she acknowledged that her roommate had significant financial resources and that her father flew in from their home state just to help her with economics homework. The participant mentioned that she called home to seek comfort from her mother about working hard and not getting the intended results. Her mom told her that she just needed to work harder, and if she did that, she would get better grades. It was that easy. Clearly frustrated by this exchange, even though it was a past incident, the participant began crying. I recalled my Mom's approach to my schoolwork and success being similar and I asked the participant if her mom was working class. "No." Was her mom a blue-collar worker? Yes. I explained that her mother was giving advice based on her own experience as a blue-collar worker. She was trained with her colleagues to do the same job. If someone worked a double shift and took on extra work, they got paid more. It would be reasonable, then, for her mother to assume that the same was true of homework. If you work harder, you get paid better (in terms of grades). But because her mom didn't have the experience of studying at a college, the concept that you could work hard and not get anywhere was a foreign concept.

Parents hold their children to high expectations and assist in meeting those goals to the best of their ability. When the resources required to meet those expectations exceed their abilities, parents seek out human resources who can help their children meet parental expectations (Antrop-González et al., 2005). While they provide support to meet parental expectations, they also talk about exceeding the accomplishments that they, as parents, have reached. Parents talk to their children about the importance of study and hard work in school for the purpose of obtaining a good job (Waterman, 2008) so that unlike themselves, children should not have to endure manual labor as a consequence for lacking a formal education (López, 2001; Waterman, 2008), and should instead be able to exceed parental levels of education (Waterman, 2008).

Demonstrating Educational Values

These high expectations are not communicated without extensive support. Through their behavior, parents show their children that education is more important than anything else and comes before any other personal, social, and even familial responsibilities. To support the standard of high expectations, successful students featured in a variety of studies reported that their parents excused them from chores, church, family obligation, visiting relatives, and holding a job while in school (Antrop-González et al., 2005; Auerbach, 2006; Ceballo, 2004, Matos, 2011). Parents further demonstrated this value of education to younger siblings by having the television turned down or by removing siblings and other distractions from the study area (Auerbach, 2006; Ceballo, 2004).

Other strategies employed by Latinx parents are "monitoring" and moral support. Parents who cannot provide the "in school" support expected by schools ensure that their children are working toward their potential through practicing the monitoring and moral support methods. Latinx families are positively empowered to influence the educational outcomes of their children by providing these support techniques that are linked to positive educational outcomes. For example, such strategies would include the discussion of schoolwork, teacher interactions, school related activities, and school performance (Woolley et al., 2009). Some parents demonstrate monitoring strategies by checking homework on a daily basis, checking their children's book bags, completing homework together, and attending meetings at school (when possible) (Antrop-González et al., 2005). The monitoring strategy also applied to external situations that pose a threat to educational attainment.

For example, through monitoring, parents safeguard their children against unsafe neighborhoods or potentially dangerous social situations and external influences (Arzubiaga, Ceja, & Artiles, 2000). The result of such monitoring is evidenced in children who perceive that their parents are monitoring their activities and friendships. These children are less likely to engage in any activity or situation that would detract from their concentration on study and school work. Personally, I was always dedicated to my studies in part, because my Mother would tell me that I'd better behave in school and work hard because I had no way of knowing when she could show up. In one particularly harrowing exchange, she once warned, "I could be sitting right behind you and you would never know it." Data show that this kind of perceived monitoring is "positively related to educational engagement" (Plunkett & Bámaca-Gómez, 2003, p. 258), and "students' self-reported grades" (p. 258). Similarly, in a study completed by Plunkett, Behnke, Sands, and Choi (2009) on "Parental Engagement and Academic Achievement in Immigrant Families," the research findings indicated that when children were aware that their mothers were utilizing the monitoring strategy, they worked harder on their schoolwork and made attempts to be better students. In a study by Antrop-González et al. (2005) on high performing Puerto Rican students, the data revealed that Puerto Rican mothers also engage in monitoring behaviors and helping their children with homework. When they can't assist with homework, they seek tutors for their children who can, which I interpret as a manifestation of social capital. Puerto Rican mothers, according to this study, also instill a deep sense of ethnic pride in their children to offset the effects of racism. This is achieved by informing their children of the realities of stereotypes and challenges that they are likely to experience as a result of their Latinx surnames. It has been documented that this practice provides Latinx students with a motivating tool by means of a desire to overcome and disprove these stereotypes (Antrop-González et al., 2005; Ceballo, 2004).

Impact of Latinx Parental Engagement on Academic Outcomes

Latinx methods and interpretations of engagement (i.e., motivation, moral support, *consejos*, and monitoring) are effective tools in supporting, enhancing, and promoting positive educational outcomes for their children. The role that the Latinx family plays in the educational outcomes of students is also crucial to positive Latinx student academic outcomes. Scholars who have studied factors that are attributed to Latinx academic success (Antrop-González et al., 2005; Cerballo, 2004; Rivera, 1997) have written that the consistent factor for positive educational outcomes for Latinx students is the significance of their family in their lives. Although Latinx parental involvement does not mirror White, middle-class involvement and is "invisible" to schools serving Latinxs, these parenting methods are meaningful.

Studies by Antrop-González et al., (2005), Ceballo (2004), and Rivera (1997) used qualitative research methods to interview high achieving Latinx students on the factors attributed to their high academic achievement. In the study conducted by Antrop-González, ten high achieving Puerto Rican high school students were asked to detail the routine of their daily lives and to describe their families. Among the resources these students listed as being instrumental in their academic success, these students listed the importance that their mothers played in offering moral support for education as well as providing academic discipline. Similarly, the study conducted by Ceballo examined Latinx parenting styles that were attributed to the positive academic performance of Latinx students. Interviewing ten first-generation, U.S. born students attending Yale University, Ceballo discovered four themes that were instrumental in Latinx academic achievement. These were identified as: strong parental commitment to education; parental encouragement of independence; verbal and nonverbal demonstrations of parental support; familiarity with positive academic supports and role models. The study by Rivera specifically examined the impact of maternal variables on the positive educational outcomes of Latinx adolescents. Findings exposed that a Latinx student's home environment was a predictor of academic success.

This demonstrated commitment for education on the part of Latinx parents is internalized by students and that internalization can lead to higher academic engagement (Plunkett et al., 2009). As parents provide their youth with the encouragement to succeed in school, student homework frequency as well as student grade point averages and graduation rates increased (Martinez, DeGarmo, & Eddy, 2004). Research conducted on Latinx parental involvement finds that monitoring, moral support and assistance with schoolwork were related to "higher educational aspirations and increased academic motivation" (Woolley et al., 2009). The frequent expression of the importance of education on the part of Latinx parents is internalized by Latinx children and results in higher academic engagement (Witkow & Fuligni, 2007). Fuligni (1997) found that when parents were perceived to be conveying the message

of the importance of education, their children were more academically successful and engaged in positive educational behaviors.

Latinx students who have a record of high academic performance credit
their parents and the verbal and nonverbal support, nurturance and guidance
they dispensed for student academic work. They credit their parents for demonstrating a commitment to their education through actions such as earlier reported monitoring behaviors and removal of obstacles and distractions that would
detract from academics (Ceballo, 2004; Waterman, 2008). Latinx students are
further able to describe their parents as maintaining an absolute commitment
to education and able to relay the parental messages that the only way in which
to escape poverty is through obtaining an education (Ceballo, 2004). When
Latinx students perceived that their actions were being monitored by parents,
when parents were involved in supporting students with schoolwork and when
there were positive rewards for doing well in school, Latinx students worked
harder on homework and made concerted efforts to do well in school (Plunkett
et al., 2009). This perception of the parental value of education is internalized
by students and can lead to higher academic engagement (Fuligni, 2007). Parents consistently promoted positive messages regarding hard work, trying one's
best and persistence even in the face of low grades (Antrop-González et al.,
2005). Students are also able to identify the concrete strategies employed by
parents such as helping students with schoolwork and when limitations restrict-
ed this assistance, noting that parents sought out appropriate resources for their
children (Antrop-González et al., 2005). In a study conducted by Rolón in
2000, the ten high-achieving Puerto Rican students' interviews perceived their
parents to be the primary driving force in their academic success and aspired to
do well in life so as to become a positive role model for their families (Antrop-
González et al., 2005). Further, students reported that they tried their best to do
well in school because they felt compelled to make their parents proud of them
by being good students and getting good grades, and they commented that their
parents operated in the capacities of friends and mentors in times of need and
crisis (Antrop-González et al., 2005).

Specifically related to education, when students believe that their parents
are able to dispense advice about school and educational endeavors, they view
their parents as educational role models and perceive that their parents value
education (Plunkett et al., 2009). Advice dispensed in the form of *consejos*
enable students to view this advice as instrumental in navigating instances of
"cultural assault" and rely on *consejos* as a means of support and strength in
enduring episodes of oppression (Espinoza-Herold, 2007).

Impact of Master Narratives on Parent/Teacher Relationships

Latinx parents are involved in the academic lives and the academic experiences of their children. However, when this manifestation of engagement does not reflect the white, middle-class representations of involvement as defined in the 1920s, Latinx parental engagement is imperceptible to schools and teachers. The intangibility of Latinx parental support renders this support invisible because it takes place within the home and outside of the auspices of the school (Auerbach, 2006).

The lack of understanding regarding Latinx parental engagement influences the ways in which teachers view Latinx parents and the assumptions that are then made about Latinx parents and perceptions regarding how much (or little) they value education. Many teachers maintain negative stereotypes about Latinx parents and portray them as apathetic, uncaring and uninvolved in regard to the education of their children. These negative viewpoints impact the interaction between teachers and parents in condescending ways (Ceballo, 2004).

During a year-long 2000–2001 study at two elementary schools in Southern California, researchers Quiocho and Daoud (2006) reported on teacher perceptions of Latinx parental involvement. In answering the first question "How can we improve parent participation at this school?" teachers responded:

- They don't come to school to help in the classroom.
- We try but we can't get them here.
- They don't and can't help in the classrooms.
- They are illiterate.
- They don't help their children with homework.
- They don't make sure their children complete their homework every night.
- They take their children to Mexico for almost anything throughout the school year and keep them away for weeks. How can the children learn this way?
- This neighborhood and this school have really changed. This used to be a good neighborhood. The professional people have moved and now we have this influx of Mexicans.
- They just don't care as much as the other parents do.

In answering the second question, "What do you see as obstacles to the academic progress of students?" teachers responded:

- Parents don't help them with their homework.
- Parents don't speak English, so they can't help.
- Kids leave for vacations and they don't do any work we assign when they are gone.
- Children don't work as hard as the other students. The students start from a different place in literacy.

Clearly lacking a cultural awareness and understanding of the realities of the values of Latinx parents in regard to education, many of the listed responses and assumptions were dispelled when teachers acquired first-hand knowledge of parents' home during home visits. Teachers who reported visiting the home of Latinx parents and took the time to learn about their Latinx students changed their initial reported perceptions (Quiocho & Daoud, 2006).

Parents who participated in this study were also asked the same questions about parental involvement and obstacles to positive educational outcomes. In the first question, "What can we do to improve parent participation?" Parents responded (in Spanish):

- Better or improved communication between teachers and parents.
- Workshops that help parents understand children's school work
- Make sure that parents understand the work that children are assigned (at home and in school).
- Personally invite parents (to come to school activities or to conferences) through phone calls.
- Use words such as "urgent" or "important" when contacting parents about school matters.
- Teacher has to be more friendly and accessible.

When asked the second question, "What are some obstacles encountered in the learning and success of your student?" Responses were as follows:

- Lack of help with homework at home.
- Transition from Spanish to English without help.
- Consistency in grades students receive from teachers.
- More attention and patience from the teacher.
- Students are confused when there are two teachers (in a team-teacher setting).

- Teachers need to keep their promises to students to reward them for doing well academically.

Latinx parents expressed a need for consistent and clear communication and a desire for personal and personable communication. Teachers and school administrators would be more effective in educating Latinx students specifically by understanding such needs and by gaining an awareness of the realities of Latinx parents and families in the United States. While teachers and administrators criticize Latinx parents for a perceived lack of involvement, they do not realize that Latinx parents tend to avoid coming to school for a variety of reasons such as the school lacking Spanish-speaking staff to logistical barriers as well as personal barriers of discomfort and shame in dealing with educators (Gándara, 1995; Romo & Falbo, 1996). Cultural norms for Latinxs dictate that they defer to teachers when it comes to their child's classroom activities and environment (Plunkett et al., 2009).

Logistical considerations, such as heavy work schedules, a need for child care and transportation also prevent Latinx parents from attending school events. Schools continually marginalize this population by lacking an awareness of their needs, failing to accommodate those needs and the inability to foster a welcoming, inviting, and inclusive environment (Delgado-Gaitán & Trueba, 1991; Fine, 1993; Lareau & Horvat, 1999).

While schools perceive engagement as being one way and while Latinx parents are unaware of what schools expect from them, there will constantly be miscommunication and missed opportunities. Latinx parents are capable of meeting the expectations of the school if they are fully apprised of what is expected of them. They misunderstand the school's perception of what involvement means because they are not aware of how the school defines engagement (Valdés, 1996). When parents are made aware of what they are being held accountable for, they become more active in their children's education, increase contact with teachers, attend more school events and offer even greater at-home support (Chrispeels & Rivero, 2001).

Note

1. This was a pattern found in my dissertation data.

References

Antrop-Gonzalez, R., Velez, W., & Garrett, T. (2005). Donde estan los estudiantes Puertorriquenos/os exitosos? [Where are the academically successful Puerto Rican students?]: Success factors of high-achieving Puerto Rican high school students. *Journal of Latinos & Education, 4*(2), 77–94.

Arellano, A., & Padilla, A. (1996). Academic invulnerability among a selected group of Latino university students. *Hispanic Journal of Behavioral Sciences, 18*(4), 485–507.

Arzubiaga, A., Ceja, M., & Artiles, A. (2000). Transcending deficit thinking about latinos' parenting styles: Toward an ecocultural view of family life. In C. Martinez, Z. Leonardo, & C. Tejeda (Eds.), *Charting new terrains of Chicana(o)/Latina(o) education* (pp. 93–106). Cresskill, NJ: Hampton Press.

Ascher, C. (1988). Improving the school-home connection for poor and minority urban students. *Urban Review, 20*(2), 109–123.

Auerbach, S. (2006). "If the student is good, let him fly": Moral support for college among Latino immigrant parents. *Journal of Latinos & Education, 5*(4), 275–292.

Azmitia, M., Cooper, C. R., Garcia, E. E., & Dunbar, N. D. (1996). The ecology of family guidance in low-income Mexican-American and European-American families. *Social Development, 5*, 1–23.

Behnke, A. O., Piercy, K. W., & Diversi, M. (2004). Educational and occupational aspirations of Latino youth and their parents. *Hispanic Journal of Behavioral Sciences, 26*(1), 16–35.

Berger, E. H. (1991). Parent involvement: Yesterday and today. *The Elementary School Journal, 91*(3), 209—219.

Carger, C. I. (1997). Attending to new voices. *Educational Leadership, 54*(7), 39–43.

Ceballo, R. (2004). From barrios to Yale: The role of parenting strategies in Latino families. *Hispanic Journal of Behavioral Sciences, 26*(2), 171–186.

Chavkin, N. F. (1991). *Family lives and parental involvement in migrant students' education.* ERIC Clearinghouse on Rural Education and Small Schools. (ERIC Document Reproduction Service No. EDO-RC-91-3).

Chavkin, N. F. (1993). *Families and schools in a pluralistic society.* New York, NY: State University of New York Press.

Chavkin, N. F., & Gonzalez, D. L. (1995). *Forging partnerships between Mexican American parents and the schools.* Charleston, WV: ERIC Clearinghouse on Rural Education and Small Schools. (ERIC Document Reproduction Service No. ED382412).

Child Trends Data Bank. (2018). *Parent involvement in schools.* https://www.childtrends.org/indicators/parental-involvement-in-schools

Chrispeels, J., & Rivero, E. (2001). Engaging Latino families for student success: How parent education can reshape parents' sense of place in the education of their children. *Peabody Journal of Education, 76*(2), 119–169.

De Gaetano, Y. (2007). The role of culture in engaging Latino parents' involvement in school. *Urban Education, 42*(2), 145–162.

Delgado-Gaitán, C. (1994). *Consejos*: The power of cultural narratives. *Anthropology & Education Quarterly, 25*(3), 298–316.

Delgado-Gaitán, C., & Trueba, H. (1991). *Crossing cultural borders: Education for immigrant families in America*. (ERIC Document Reproduction Service No. ED334318).

Espinosa, L. M. (1995). *Hispanic parent involvement in early childhood programs*. Champaign, IL: ERIC Clearinghouse on Elementary and Early Childhood Education. (ERIC Document Reproduction Service No. ED382412).

Espinoza-Herold, M. (2007). Stepping beyond si se puede: Dichos as a cultural resource in mother-daughter interaction in a Latino family. *Anthropology & Education Quarterly, 38*(3), 260–277.

Epstein, J. L. (1996). Perspectives and previews in research and policy for school, family, and community partnerships. In A. Booth & J. F. Dunn (Eds.), *Family-school links* (pp. 209–246). Mahwah, NJ: Erlbaum.

Fine, M. (1993). [Ap]parent involvement: Reflections on parents, power, and urban public schools. *Teachers College Record, 94*(4), 682–709.

Floyd, L. (1998). Joining hands: A parental involvement program. *Urban Education, 33*(1), 123–135.

Fuligni, A. (1997). The academic achievement of adolescents from immigrant families: The roles of family background, attitudes, and behavior. *Child Development, 68*(2), 351–363.

Harding, N. N. (2006). Ethnic and social class similarities and differences in mothers' beliefs about kindergarten preparation. *Race, Ethnicity & Education, 9*(2), 223–237.

Gándara, P. (1995). *Over the ivy wall: The educational mobility of low-income Chicanos*. Albany, NY: State University of New York Press.

Goldenberg, C., & Gallimore, R. (1995). Immigrant Latino parents' values and beliefs about their children's education: Continuities and discontinuities across cultures and generations. *Advances in Motivation and Achievement, 9*, 183–228.

Halgunseth, L., Ispa, J., & Rudy, D. (2006). Parental control in Latino families: An integrated review of the literature. *Child Development, 77*(5), 1282–1297.

Lara-Alecio, R., Irby, B., & Ebener, R. (1997). Developing academically supportive behaviors among Hispanic parents: What elementary teachers and administrators can do. *Preventing School Failure, 42*(1), 27–32.

Lareau, A., & Horvat, E. (1999). Moments of social inclusion: Race, class, and cultural capital in family school relationships. *Sociology of Education, 71*, 39–56.

López, G. (2001). The value of hard work: Lessons on parent involvement from an (im)migrant household. *Harvard Education Review, 71*(3), 416–437.

Martinez, C., DeGarmo, D., & Eddy, J. (2004). Promoting academic success among Latino youth. *Hispanic Journal of Behavioral Sciences, 26*(2), 128–151.

Matos, J. M. D. (2011). *Fulfilling their dreams: Latina/o college student narratives on the impact of parental involvement on their academic engagement*. (Unpublished doctoral dissertation). University of Massachusetts, Amherst, MA.

Mehan, H., Villanueva, I., Hubbard, L., & Lintz, A. (1996). *Constructing school success: The consequences of untracking low-achieving students*. New York, NY: Cambridge University Press.

Moles, O., D'Angelo, D., & Office of Educational Research and Improvement (ED). (1993). *Building school-family partnerships for learning: Workshops for urban educators.* (ERIC Document Reproduction Service No. ED364651).

Moll, L., Amanti, C., Neff, D., & Gonzalez, N. (1992). Funds of knowledge for teaching: Using a qualitative approach to connect homes and classrooms. *Theory into Practice, 31*(1), 132–141.

Okagaki, L., & Frensch, P. (1998). Parenting and children's school achievement: A multiethnic approach. *American Educational Research Journal, 35*(1), 123–144.

Peterson, D. (1989). *Parent involvement in the educational process.* Eugene, OR: ERIC Clearinghouse on Educational Management. (ERIC Document Reproduction Service No. ED312776).

Plunkett, S., & Bámaca-Gómez, M. (2003). The relationship between parenting, acculturation, and adolescent academics in Mexican-origin immigrant families in Los Angeles. *Hispanic Journal of Behavioral Sciences, 25*(2), 222–239.

Plunkett, S. W., Behnke, A. O., Sands, T., & Choi, B. Y. (2009). Adolescents' reports of parental engagement and academic achievement in immigrant families. *Journal of Youth and Adolescence, 38*(2), 257–268.

Quiocho, A., & Daoud, A. (2006). Dispelling myths about Latino parent participation in schools. *The Educational Forum, 70*(3), 255–267.

Reese, L., Balzano, S., Gallimore, R., & Goldenberg, C. (1995). The concept of educación: Latino family values and American schooling. *International Journal of Educational Research, 23*, 57–81.

Rivera, M. (1997). *Maternal factors affecting the academic achievement of Latino adolescents.* (ERIC Document Reproduction Service No. ED424011).

Romo, H. D., & Falbo, T. (1996). *Latino high school graduation: Defying the odds.* Austin, TX: University of Texas Press.

Sosa, A. S. (1997). Involving Hispanic parents in educational activities through collaborative relationships. *Bilingual Research Journal, 21*(2–3), 1–8.

Scribner, J. D., Young, M. D., & Pedroza, A. (1999). Building collaborative relationships with parents. In P. Reyes, J. D. Scribner, & A. P. Scribner (Eds.), *Lessons from high-performing Hispanic schools: Creating learning communities* (pp. 36–60). New York, NY: Teachers College Press.

Stanton-Salazar, R. D. (2001). *Manufacturing hope and despair: The school and kin support networks of capital U.S.-Mexican youth.* New York, NY: Teachers College Press.

Treviño, R. (2004). *Against all odds: Lessons from parents of migrant high achievers.* Paper presented at the Hawaii International Conference on Education, Honolulu, HI.

Trueba, H., & Delgado-Gaitán, C. (1988). *Minority achievement and parental support: Academic resocialization through mentoring.* Santa Barbara, CA: University of California.

Trumbull, E., Rothstein-Fisch, C., Greenfield, P. M., & Quiroz, B. (2001). *Bridging cultures between home and schools: A guide for teachers.* Mahwah, NJ: Erlbaum.

Valdés, G. (1996). *Con respeto: Bridging the distances between culturally diverse families and schools: An ethnographic portrait.* New York, NY: Teachers College Press.

Valencia, R. R., & Black, M. S. (2002). "Mexican Americans don't value education!"— The basis of the myth, mythmaking, and debunking. *Journal of Latinos and Education, 1*(2), 81–103.

Villenas, S., & Moreno, M. (2001). *Valerse por si Misma* between race, capitalism, and patriarchy: Latina mother-daughter pedagogies in North Carolina. *International Journal of Qualitative Studies in Education, 14*(5), 671–696.

Villanueva, I. (1996). Change in the educational life of Chicano families across three generations. *Education and Urban Society, 29*, 13–34.

Waterman, R. A. (2008). Strength behind the sociolinguistic wall: The dreams, commitments, and capacities of Mexican mothers. *Journal of Latinos and Education, 7*(2), 144–162.

Witkow, M., & Fuligni, A. (2007). Achievement goals and daily school experiences among adolescents with Asian, Latino, and European American backgrounds. *Journal of Educational Psychology, 99*(3), 584–596.

Woolley, M. E., Kol, K. L., & Bowen, G. L. (2009). The social context of school success for Latino middle school students: Direct and indirect influences of teachers, family, and friends. *Journal of Early Adolescence, 29*(1), 43–70.

Zalaquett, C. P. (2006). Study of successful Latina/o students. *Journal of Hispanic Higher Education, 5*(1), 35–47.

· 4 ·

HOW LATINX PARENTAL ENGAGEMENT
BECAME INVISIBLE

The past few chapters have included narratives about my Mother's high caliber of parental engagement. Yet, when interacting with my elementary and high schools, she was not seen as involved as the parents of my white peers. How do we make meaning out of the assertions that in this country, white parental engagement[1] is valued more than Latinx parental engagement in American schools? What theoretical frameworks can help social justice educators to contextualize how racism plays a role in whose voice is heard and whose voice is absent in the discussion of Latinx parental involvement?

I argue that these theoretical frameworks are Latino Critical Race Theory (LatCrit) and Critical Race Theory (CRT). In this chapter, I set out with four goals in mind. First, I will historically situate CRT and LatCrit. This will include tracing the origins of CRT and explaining how CRT provides a foundation for LatCrit. I begin with CRT because this is the foundation from where LatCrit gains its legitimacy. Second, to foreground the relevant principles of LatCrit, I will present the main principles of CRT and make the distinction between CRT and LatCrit. This will be accomplished by sharing the main principles of these theories and demonstrating how a LatCrit framework makes meaning out of the devaluing of Latinx parental engagement. Third, I will explain how LatCrit is applied to analyzing racial dynamics in education.

Fourth, and finally, I apply the principles and understanding of LatCrit to make meaning out of Latinx parental engagement.

There are many theoretical frameworks that could have been used as lens through which to critique the inherent racism that discredits Latinx parental engagement and holds white, middle-class parental engagement as the "standard." There are strength-based and cultural theories that explain and situate the contributions of Latinx parents in the education of their children. While these theories have their merit and unique contributions, LatCrit and CRT speak directly to the field of social justice education. As CRT deals specifically with race, LatCrit is related to social justice in that similar to social justice, it "can address the intersectionality of racism, sexism, classism, and other forms of oppression" (Solórzano & Delgado Bernal, 2001, p. 312). LatCrit and CRT are related to social justice education, and the challenge put forth by social justice education—transformation. Like social justice education,

> [CRT] contains an activist dimension. It not only tries to understand our social situation, but to change it; it sets out not only to ascertain how society organizes itself along racial lines and hierarchies, but to transform it for the better. (Delgado & Stefancic, 2001, p. 3)

Social justice is not a static field of study. It is a field of study that is alive, active, and calls upon its students to challenge the status quo, much like the doctrines supported by LatCrit and CRT. In order to understand how LatCrit and CRT can be instrumental in transformation and how they enable educators to be change agents, it is important to understand the meaning and historical positioning of these frameworks.

Origins and Principles of CRT and LatCrit

As defined by Matsuda (cited in Solórzano & Yosso, 2001), Critical Race Theory or CRT, is the theoretical framework that initially began in the field of law to examine and account for the presence of racism in American law and work toward eliminating racism[2] and all forms of oppression. CRT was initially discussed by early writers and legal scholars Richard Delgado, Derrick Bell, and Alan Freeman, in the mid-1970s (Delgado & Stefancic, 2001; Dixson & Rousseau, 2006; Yosso, 2006). It was developed as a response to the inability of Critical Legal Studies (CLS) to analyze and address race and racial injustice in U.S. law (Crenshaw, 2002; Crenshaw, Gotanda, Peller, & Thomas, 1995; DeCuir & Dixson, 2004; Delgado, 1988; Delgado & Stefancic, 2001). Initially in the field of law, CRT was criticized for focusing too heavily on the Black/ White binary. The voices of the intersections of identity and marginalization were absent from the conversations on race and oppression (Espinoza & Harris, 1998). From the field of law, it spread into other fields such as sociology, history, ethnic studies and women's studies, and witnessed the creation of Latino Critical Race Theory (LatCrit).

LatCrit expanded the conversations in CRT to include the experiences of Latinxs and Chicanxs[3] and drew into consideration the intersection of identities (Solórzano & Yosso, 2001). Through LatCrit, these scholars asserted "that racism, sexism, and classism are experienced amid other layers of subordination based on immigration status, sexuality, culture, language, phenotype, accent and surname" (Montoya, cited in Yosso, 2006, p. 170).

CRT scholars and the activists who use CRT as their basis for activist work are "interested in studying and transforming the relationship among race, racism, and power" (Delgado & Stefancic, 2001, p. 2).

CRT is driven by six principles that define the CRT movement (Matsuda, 1991). These principles are related to the application of LatCrit:

1. Critical race theory recognizes that racism is endemic to American life.
2. Critical race theory expresses skepticism toward dominant legal claims of neutrality, objectivity, colorblindness, and meritocracy.
3. Critical race theory challenges ahistoricism and insists on a contextual/ historical analysis of the law...Critical race theorists...adopt a stance that presumes that racism has contributed to all contemporary manifestations of group advantage and disadvantage.
4. Critical race theory insists on recognition of the experiential knowledge of people of color and our communities of origin in analyzing law and society.
5. Critical race theory is interdisciplinary.
6. Critical race theory works toward the end of eliminating racial oppression as part of the broader goal of ending all forms of oppression. (p. 6)

Believing that race was under-theorized in the field of education, scholars Ladson-Billings and Tate sought to fill this theoretical gap with CRT and its application to race based inequity in education. In 1994, they presented a paper at the annual meeting of the American Educational Research Association (AERA) where they asserted:

[R]ace remains a salient factor in U.S. society in general and in education in particular…In particular, building on the work of Bell and others, they detailed the intersection of race and property rights and the ways this intersection could be used to understand inequity in schools and schooling. (cited in Dixson & Rousseau, 2006, p. 5)

Utilizing CRT's six principles, LatCrit seeks to challenge the notions of
colorblindness, meritocracy, objectivity, and neutrality (Dixson & Rousseau,
2006). To issue this challenge, LatCrit scholars explore the themes of the
notion of "voice" (Delgado, 1989) and the intersection of race and property
(Harris, 1993) both of which arise out of legal discourse.

The six principles relevant to LatCrit, the notion of "voice" and the intersection of race and property are important in their relationship to the subject
of Latinx parental engagement. In order to address racism, as Justice Blackmun stated, "we must first take account of race" (*Regents of University of CA v.
Bakke*, 1978, p. 257). In addressing principle one "CRT recognizes that racism
is endemic to American life," we must examine the ways in which racism
plays a part in the race based educational malpractice being experienced by
Latinxs. Race is a social construction from a social constructionist standpoint.
While "Latinx" is not considered to be a race, but a culture in the United
States, it is a classification that has been *racialized*. As such, it is subjected to
the levels and types of oppression (Hardiman, Jackson, & Griffin, 2010) and
the maintenance of the system of racism. Latinxs experience racism through
agents of oppression and conscious and unconscious acts and on the individual, institutional, and cultural level (Hardiman et al., 2010). A sample of how
Latinxs might experience levels and types of oppression is detailed in Table
4.1.

Table 4.1: Examples of levels and types of oppression for Latinx students.

	Individual	Institutional	Cultural
Conscious	Teacher expects students to assimilate into mainstream culture and practices.	State-mandated anti-bilingual education policies.	Latinxs are expected to speak English and penalized for speaking Spanish.
Unconscious	Teachers assume that Latinx parents do not care about the education of their children.	Latinx student is placed in a lower track because of language proficiency.	Teachers accept and believe the norm that the best way for a Latinx child to succeed is through assimilation.

Source: Author.

Principle two challenges the notions of colorblindness and meritocracy. According to NCES (2013), "Latinos have one or more full-time security guards compared to 29% of all public schools. Latinxs are also subjected to more in-school arrests (37%) than their African American (35%) and white (21%) counterparts." What stands out in these data is not a notion of color-*blindness* but a very focused lens on the issue of color and race. LatCrit is skeptical of the notion of meritocracy and rightly so. The notion of meritocracy pertains to the Horatio Alger "American" work ethic belief that every American can succeed by "pulling himself up from his bootstraps." In order for someone to be able to pull themselves up from their bootstraps, they first need to have access to boots, then they must be allowed to acquire the boots. This is a "myth of meritocracy" (Love, 2004, p. 229) because it assumes that all citizens have equal access to resources. According to the Pew Research Center (2017), as of 2015, Latinxs made up 67% of the workforce but their median annual household income was only $44,800, and almost 22% were living in poverty. The third principle of CRT, one that proposes that the system of racism has contributed to present-day manifestations of advantage and disadvantage, is correlated to the introduction of race and property by Harris (1993). To summarize, Harris analyzes whiteness as "property" and describes the "property functions of whiteness" (Dixson & Rousseau, 2006, p. 22). She details these property functions in three parts. The first among these are the rights of disposition; two, rights to use and enjoyment; and three, the absolute right to exclude.

Rights and Privileges Afforded by Whiteness

The "right of disposition"[4] asserts that property is alienable, and whiteness is valued property (Harris, 1993). In other words, it is that which can be transferred to another's ownership (Merriam-Webster, 1991). Although one cannot bestow whiteness or the benefits of whiteness to someone who is non-white. Even the concept of someone being "non-white" normalizes and organizes whiteness into a privileged state. A person of color can benefit from conforming to white norms. More tangibly put, consider whiteness as a house you (i.e., a white person) couldn't sell, but person of color could benefit from living in. Rewards are given for compliance to white standards. Transferring this application of the concept to Latinx parents, Latinx parents who adhere to "white norms" and the white standard of parental engagement are rewarded and touted as being involved and caring parents. On the other hand, Latinx parents who instead adhere to their own cultural norms of parenting are viewed as uncaring and uninvolved in the educational outcomes of their children. Similar to what is seen when someone does not follow the cycle of socialization (Harro, 2008), the consequence for not assimilating to white standards is met with sanctioning.

As documented by various scholars, whiteness comes with privilege (McIntosh, 1990; Tatum, 2017; Wildman & Davis, 2000). Following the idea that whiteness is a house, there are privileges that determine the "rights to use and enjoyment" with owning that house. For instance, there are economic privileges associated with owning the house. The house's mortgage can be refinanced to fund a child's college education, the house can be sold to buy a better house, the house's location can afford access to good schools with advanced placement offerings or even better-quality teachers. Considering how rights to use and enjoyment, not having these privileges by virtue of being a person of color (in this case, Latinx) could mean that your child is put in a "low track" because of a lack of mastery of the English language; there are no specialists to work with your child to enter a higher track, which leads to the third and final property function, the right to exclude.

By owning whiteness, and by owning the house, the homeowner has the "absolute right to exclude" and to decide who can enter and who cannot; who is welcomed and who is not. Currently, in the governmental push to build a border wall between the U.S. and Mexico, we are deciding who is allowed to trespass those borders. During the period of racial segregation, people of color were excluded altogether. With the decision in *Plessy v. Ferguson* (1896), the right to exclude was even sanctioned by the law. The current manifestations of exclusion lay with such sanctioned and underground segregation as white flight, schools of choice, vouchers, charter schools and magnet schools. Latinx children would be excluded from a magnet school, for example, if they were unable to pass the admissions testing. Latinx parents would be excluded and unable to help their children gain access to such a school if they lacked the cultural capital[5] to do so.

The fourth principle of CRT which acknowledges experiential learning is also connected to the notion of "voice" as it is an important theme in LatCrit. It is one deeply embedded in LatCrit that facilitates "counter storytelling," that which was initially used to offer a contextual and historical analysis of the law, but which can also be applied in education. "Voice" is the "assertion and acknowledgement of the importance of the personal and the community experiences of people of color as sources of knowledge" (Dixson & Rousseau, 2006, p. 35). Through the affirmation of the counter stories told by marginalized groups, master narratives can be challenged, the silence and "othering" experienced by people of color can be given voice, and within that voice, a means to combat racism (Delgado & Stefancic, 2001). In my college course on racism and inequality in schools and society, I take the chalk while writing and reciting the following on the chalkboard "In 1492, Columbus…" U.S.-educated students will proudly sing in unison "sailed the ocean blue!" and they always seem a bit pleased with themselves for knowing this, for being able to recite the master narrative. I smile back at them and turn again to the chalkboard, once again writing and reciting "In 1493, Columbus…" and I am met with silence because for many, they have not learned the counter-narrative of Taínos and marginalized groups exploited and worse by Columbus. I tell them that the counter-narrative would be "In 1493, Columbus stole all that he could see." U.S. history books can also serve as hostile environments for students of color, retraumatizing and recolonizing their experience as students. When I share what the history books omitted, some of my students express feeling hurt, betrayed, and angry.

Defining LatCrit as a tool with which to combat racism is further expounded and explored by scholars who study LatCrit and its application in education. It is where principles five and six of CRT are explained more comprehensively.

CRT and LatCrit Defined in Education

CRT as defined by scholars Solórzano and Yosso (2001) extends the definition by Matsuda to say:

> "[CRT seeks to] develop a pedagogy, curriculum, and research agenda that accounts for the role of race and racism in U.S. education and to work toward the elimination of racism as part of a larger goal of eliminating all forms of subordination in education" (p. 3) They go on to define the application of CRT in the field of education as "an attempt to link theory with practice, scholarship with teaching, and the academy with the community." (p. 3)

CRT as defined here by Solórzano and Yosso argues that critical race methodology in education hold five elements that inform perspectives and methodologies in schools. They introduce these as: the intercentricity of race and racism with other forms of subordination, the challenge to dominant ideology, the commitment to social justice, the centrality of experiential knowledge, and the transdisciplinary perspective. Solórzano and Yosso discuss the themes of majoritarian storytelling in American schools and how it privileges the dominant ideology. They contend that one of the ways to combat majoritarian storytelling is by introducing methods of counter-storytelling.

The theoretical model as defined by Solórzano and Yosso maintains that in order to understand the mechanizations of race and racism as they are manifested in schools, we must also address the ways in which there is also an intersection of identities (gender and class are two examples most salient in the relevant research), that further complicate race and racism in schools and by examining the intersections of identity for people of color (in this case, I argue Latinxs), we can more accurately speak to a fuller picture of the experience of Latinxs. As a college faculty member who also identifies as first-generation and with a multiplicity of identities, I can see how magnified the experiences of students of color are on campus, especially on Predominantly White Institutions (PWIs). First-generation Latinx students have to navigate the unfamiliar terrain of the campus and college norms and traditions as well as navigating this territory as a person of color. They have to hold their identities as first-generation *and* a person of color while trying to survive and thrive in college. If they are on work-study through a financial aid package, they have to balance being first-generation, wading through racism, and serving the college with less time to study as their non-first generation, white, middle and upper class peers.

While school systems would like to hold fast to the claim that they are institutions that are merit based, race neutral and colorblind, LatCrit challenges that notion by confronting white privilege and questions deficit theory that skews the perceptions held of people of color (Solórzano & Yosso, 2001). Specifically, this privilege is challenged with the argument that if schools participate in ways that can be used to marginalize and oppress people of color and people who identify with traditionally subordinated groups, then schools can alternately employ methods to empower and liberate. With that understanding, LatCrit and the manifestation of LatCrit in pedagogy and practice strives to enact social justice and strives to achieve a liberatory consciousness (Love, 2000).

In order to achieve a liberatory consciousness, one needs to be aware of the systems of oppression at play around them, be able to analyze the system, decided to take action, and hold themselves and their peer social identity group, accountable for transgressions. If deficit theorists are willing to claim that Latinx parents are a deficit to the education of their children, how likely would they be to claim that there is an importance and legitimacy in the experiential knowledge of people of color and instrumental in teaching about understanding and analysis of racial oppression? LatCrit views this knowledge as a strength and incorporates cultural strategies like oral storytelling such as sharing *dichos, cuentos* and *refranes* (i.e., advice shared through narratives) in highlighting this experiential knowledge (Solórzano & Yosso, 2001). Similar to the belief in the importance of recognizing and analyzing the intersections of identity for people of color, the emphasis on a transdisciplinary perspective calls for an intersection of scholarly disciplines to situate race and racism in historical and contemporary locations.

In their work, Solórzano and Yosso are fully apprised of the reality that while no one of these themes is unique, collectively they can be utilized to challenge deficit models of scholarship. The argument in incorporating this element is that it also advances the ability of people of color to understand the frameworks that construct the arguments against them and by understanding these frameworks, they are further prepared to defend themselves against systems of oppression.

One of the defenses against forms of racial oppression is through the utilization of counter-storytelling against majoritarian storytelling. Similar to the work of Love (2004), Solórzano and Yosso (2001) propose that majoritarian storytelling maintains the advantage of white privilege. If the story of the dominant society is the only story being told, and the dominant practice of storytelling is the "standard," it creates invisibility on the part of stories in subordinated societies and makes the dominant (white, middle-class) story, the "normal" majoritarian story. One explanation for this is the use of Bourdieu's (Bourdieu & Passeron, 1977) concept of cultural capital. The notion of cultural capital refers to a type of cultural wealth held by members of dominant groups. In the theory of cultural capital, Bourdieu asserts that that three types of capital (cultural, social, and economic)[6], can be obtained in one of two ways. It can be acquired through one's family (lineage, heritage, inheritance, etc.) or it could be gained through formal education. Subordinated groups experience exclusion from this capital as the only way to obtain it is through acquisition of wealth or access into education, a field in which they are disenfranchised. Yosso (2006) critiques the use of Bourdieu's theory of cultural capital as it has been used to explain the achievement gap between white students and students of color to claim "some communities are culturally wealthy while others are culturally poor" (Yosso, 2006). This explanation is seen through a superficial lens that does not, as LatCrit would have it, analyze the system and maintenance of racism and the subordination of Latinxs at play. It also connects to the notion of master and counter narratives and who gets to define what it means to be "culturally wealthy" or "culturally poor." It therefore goes back to Harris's property functions of whiteness where the "interpretation of Bourdieu exposes White, middle-class culture as the standard, and therefore all other forms and expressions of 'culture' are judged in comparison to this 'norm'" (Yosso, 2006, p. 174). This offers a possible explanation to why Latinx parenting styles are devalued and strengthens the argument for the importance and necessity of counter stories. Counter-stories allow for action and empowerment on the part of traditionally marginalized groups. In discussing the empowerment of Latinx parents, I use a LatCrit lens with which we can see and understand these counter stories.

Understanding Latinx Parental Engagement Through a LatCrit Lens

Through counter storytelling and the recognition of experiential knowledge, the application of LatCrit acknowledges that people who identify with communities of color (in this case, Latinx people), also have various types of capital. The nature of racism and the property value of whiteness, as discussed earlier, render this capital invisible because it is not the "norm." People of color do possess capital in at least six forms that are related to the ways in which Latinx parents are engaged in the education of their children. These six forms are: aspirational, navigational, social, linguistic, familial, and resistance (Auerbach, 2001; Delgado Bernal, 1997; Faulstich Orellana, 2003; Solórzano & Delgado Bernal, 2001; Stanton-Salazar, 2001). Similar to the acknowledgement of CRTs notion of intersectionality, these six forms are interconnected. For example, if a Latinx parent encourages his or her child to overcome obstacles with the adage "¡Si se puede!" they are manifesting *aspirational capital* by encouraging children to hold on to their hopes and dreams despite obstacles; *navigational capital* by fortifying children with inner resources and resilience that empower their children to endure stressful events and hostile environments; *social capital* by utilizing social networks to obtain resources needed for their children to experience positive educational outcomes; *linguistic capital* by the tradition of storytelling evidenced through the sharing of *consejos*, *dichos*, and *refranes*, a style of storytelling in the Latinx tradition that imparts to the storyteller the skills of "memorization, attention to detail, dramatic pauses, comedic timing, facial affect, vocal tone, volume, rhythm and rhyme" (Yosso, 2006, p. 177); *familial capital* through family members who are either directly related by blood, community, or friendship. The members of the family and the extended family also model for children important cultural mores such as *educación* (Delgado-Gaitán, 1994, 2001; Elenes, Gonzalez, Delgado Bernal, & Villenas, 2001). These lessons imparted by family inform a student's consciousness on the emotional, occupational, moral, and educational level (Auerbach, 2006; Elenes et al., 2001; Lopez, 2003; Reese, 1992); and *resistance capital* by teaching children the skills of oppositional behavior to challenge inequality (Delgado Bernal, 1997; Freire, 1970; Giroux, 1983; Solórzano & Delgado Bernal, 2001). Latinx parents do this, as mentioned in section two of this paper, by teaching their children about racism and cultural pride in the face of such oppression. In turn, as supported by data, children strive to do well in school to prove these negative cultural notions wrong (Antrop-Gonzalez et al., 2005). Latinx parents are impacting the educational experiences of their children by affording them with these six forms of capital. Educational institutions can also have a more positive impact on the educational outcomes of Latinx children by incorporating the principles of LatCrit into the educational process.

Suggestions for Including LatCrit in Education

CRT aims to keep race at the center of a critique of the educational malpractice perpetuated by academic institutions and to further this critique with the active process of social change (DeCuir & Dixson, 2004). LatCrit, in particular, keeps Latinx issues and the intersectionality of these issues at the center of this critique (Solórzano & Yosso, 2001). By attesting to the importance of one of the principles of CRT, counter storytelling, the once "othered" voices of marginalized Latinx parents and their children can challenge the ahistoricism of the privileged "norm."

A means by which educational institutions can work to challenge the notion of the "norm" is through a process of anti-oppressive education that, as stated by Kumashiro (2000), acknowledges that schools can perpetuate oppression but have the ability to perpetuate liberation and liberatory practices by incorporating, and not by exoticizing the voices and the experiences of the "other." In regard to Latinx parents, property can be shared in the acknowledgement that there is no one, single "truth," nor one single norm. Privileges need not be withheld from Latinx parents for not adhering to the White, middle-class standard of parenting. Realizing the contributions afforded by the unique styles of Latinx parental engagement, Latinxs would no longer be excluded from the use and enjoyment of privileged spaces. Appreciating the fact that Latinxs also possess capital and linguistic capital removes the stigma and sanctions of bilingual education and confers legitimization of the linguistic skills that Latinx parents teach their children and the skills that these children bring to their classrooms.

Through incorporating Latinx perspectives in the utilization of storytelling, appreciating Latinx parental engagement as a valued practice, and by incorporating the voices and experiential learning of traditionally marginalized students, these students can rise from the sidelines of passive consumerism to take part in their education as active participants (hooks, 1994) seeing themselves and their families reflected in the curriculum (Kumashiro, 2000) and their learning taking on new meanings of relevance. The analysis of whiteness as property, the right to exclude and the analysis of privilege can reveal the construction and "norming" of whiteness and White parental involvement as the norm, facilitate a discourse on the manner in which whiteness remained the norm (thereby excluding Latinx parents) and lead to the activist engagement of dismantling racist social constructions.

The construct of parental engagement as we know it today (i.e., attending PTA meetings, volunteering at your children's schools, showing up to parent/teacher conferences and school plays) have dominated the discourse regarding parental engagement, creating a majoritarian story (Love, 2000) that there is only one way of parenting that is supported by a larger social construct. This larger social construction of what successful parental engagement looks like omits, silences, marginalizes, and makes invisible, other populations of parents whose parenting styles are effective, but not valued, because it is not the dominant means of parenting (Harris, 1993; Yosso, 2006). One such disenfranchised group is Latinx parents.

In spite of deficit theorizing that paints a portrait of Latinx parents as being uninvolved and disinterested in the academic performance of their children, qualitative and quantitative data support the fact that Latinx parents are not only actively engaged in the education of their children, but that their parenting styles transmit this value of education. Further, the pedagogical approaches of Latinx parents have a positive impact on the educational outcomes of their children in their academic performance and occupational and educational aspirations. These pedagogical approaches are manifested through cultural values that place a strong emphasis on the value of an education and differentiate between a dominant view of education and a Latinx cultural value of *educación*. Latinx parents teach that school is important, remove distractions that serve as obstacles to obtaining an education, help with homework, impart that the teacher's role is one to be respected, and teach the importance of good manners and good behavior in school and with figures of authority. Imagine what could be possible for Latinx youth—and all under-represented groups in education—if schools partnered with parents.

While data support the high level with which Latinx parents are engaged and invested in the education of their children, this engagement goes unseen. The work of LatCrit and CRT theorists offer a framework with which we can understand the dynamics that perpetuates the invisibility of the contributions of Latinx parents to the positive educational outcomes of their children. For example, the work of Harris (1993) on whiteness as property can be applied to understand how the dominant view of parental engagement has become the model for what parental engagement looks like. When whiteness is val-ued property with value only transferrable to members of dominant groups or members of marginalized groups who assimilate to dominant practices, there is little room for the Latinx voice to be heard or for that voice and that insight to hold value. When dominant groups have the ability to enjoy and utilize re-sources in ways that are recognizable and sanctioned by the dominant group, there seems to be little room for Latinxs to utilize, claim, or have equal access to those resources. When the dominant group has the absolute right to ex-clude subordinated groups, Latinxs have little opportunity to be seen or heard as contributing members to the field of parental engagement. As referred to in chapter two, the notion of parental engagement in education did not have a focus on parents and communities of color, but at its inception, had the inter-ests of white, middle-class parents at the center. It is here that one of Pharr's *Common Elements of Oppression* (lack of prior claim) can be applied (Pharr, 1995). In other words, since Latinx parents weren't present at the original discussions and design for parental engagement, they do not have the right to a present claim of how parents can be regarded as "engaged." While a critique of this analysis might suggest that this analysis depicts a bleak and hopeless scenario, the contrary is true.

A LatCrit framework poses that there is hope for the transformation of how school systems envision parental engagement because schools can take active measures to incorporate counter storytelling in the curriculum, practice and pedagogy. The principles of LatCrit and the practice and pedagogy of Lat-inx parenting coalesce to create a *new* framework and vision on how to rede-sign the notion of parental engagement for all parents. LatCrit and CRT can assist with framing this redesign in their practice of keeping race, a critique of racism and suggestions for activism at the fore. LatCrit and CRTs ability to see—and not see through—race, forces educators and educational systems to question and critique the ways in which schools are harmful places (Kumashiro, 2000). These frameworks also problematize expectations of assimilation that ask that Latinxs fit the schools and not confronting schools to change the ways that they work with Latinx parents. Accepting and analyzing that race impacts educational practices and policies allows educators to note the groups are advantaged and disadvantaged based on racial categories. White parents who are involved in the education of their children have a positive impact on the educational outcomes of their children. The same is true for Latinx parents, but they are not valued in the same way, and the common denominator by no coincidence, happens to be a U.S. categorization of race. When LatCrit and CRT challenge the notion that we live in a colorblind society, these frameworks simultaneously offer educators a new way to see, consider, and value parental engagement. Just as there is no one, widely accepted definition of parental engagement, there is no one, sole, universal way for parents to be engaged. This consideration invites Latinx parental engagement into a dialogue that they have been excluded from for far too long. Inviting Latinx parents into a dialogue on their understanding of parental engagement has shown to yield learning environments where Latinx parents and school systems are equal partners in the education of Latinx students (Delgado-Gaitán, 2001).

Utilization of principles of LatCrit and CRT into educational practices and policies help educators to better understand Latinx parents and their children. For example, storytelling, a long-standing Latinx tradition, creates space for Latinx parents to share their experiences in a manner that evidences their expertise, and to be received in a manner where their voices are heard. Storytelling would enable Latinx parents to share how they feel they are involved in the education of their children (i.e., they are helping the classroom teacher by teaching their children to be respectful, reaching for not just an education, but *una buena educacíon*, checking homework, helping with homework or seeking help for their children with their schoolwork). In turn, listening to the stories of Latinx parents allows for educators to note that Latinx parents are not uninvolved in the education of their children, they are solely *differently* involved.

The power of the utilization of the principles of LatCrit has been realized in successful partnerships between schools and parents. One instance is in Carpenteria, a small community in California, where the *Comité de Padres Latinos* (COPLA) was formed in the 1970s by Latinx parents. The group was formed in an effort to generate more parental participation in their school communities. The organization of COPLA embodies the issues faced by Latinx parents (i.e., miscommunication between Latinx parents and the schools; misunderstanding of Latinx parents and culture; ill-prepared teachers who are not cognizant of Latinx parenting styles). Parents didn't know how to engage with the schools and teachers were mistaking perceived inaction as an indication that the parents of Carpenteria didn't care about the educational outcomes of their children. The teachers in the community lacked the training necessary to understand the cultural differences between how Latinx parenting was different from the norm, and Latinx parents were frustrated by the personal limitations (communication and literacy skills) and their confusion about the school system. Not understanding that it wasn't a Latinx parenting issue, but a structural one, at the root of the problem, Latinx parents blamed themselves for their children's academic underperformance (Delgado-Gaitán, 2001). Today, the teachers are aware, sensitive, and attuned to the essence of Latinx parenting in regard to educational engagement. The parents are better informed about the school system and what is expected of them from the school. Together in this understanding, each works in partnership with the other where Latinx parents created channels through which they could be heard and where teachers translate the notices that are sent home. To get to this point, parents and school personnel engaged in dialogue where the school was able to identify and explain their expectations regarding parental engagement. In turn, with a shared understanding, parents were able to meet those expectations and share their narrative of parental engagement and how that engagement is manifested culturally.

While LatCrit and CRT frameworks and applications are powerful, they have been met with criticism as well. In regard to the tenet of storytelling, the critiques state that these counter stories take liberties with the truth and that this kind of narrative stifles debate and discussion because it places the subordinated in a better position to make arguments because of their lived experiences (Delgado & Stefancic, 2001; Dixson & Rousseau, 2006). The storytelling tenet is also critiqued for lacking intellectual rigor and therefore, making the analysis of storytelling, difficult (Farber & Sherry, 1993; Posner, 1995; Tushnet, 1992). Critics also take what they call the "voice of color" and "standing" to task, taking issue with CRT claiming that they are better equipped with the experience necessary to understand issues of people of color because of their race (whereas white scholars are ill-prepared to do so). The response to this critique on the part of LatCrit and CRT has been that while white scholars should not be disqualified from having a dialogue about issues pertaining to people of color, these issues are "often better addressed by minorities" taking into consideration the stage of consciousness of the "minority" (Delgado & Stefancic, 2001, p. 92). The critique of CRT storytelling and assessing the validity of one group's truth over another is met with the CRT response that "truth is a social construct created to suit the purposes of the dominant group" and establishing one universal truth, be it the truth of the dominant or the subordinated is difficult to ascertain (p. 92).

Limitations within the research on Latinx parental engagement is related to the growth of the Latinx population. Since the population is growing and changing, every scenario regarding Latinx parents could not have been anticipated. This leaves a gap in the research that allows for further questioning and inquiry. One such limitation in the research is how Latinx parents are defined. The literature refers to Latinx *parents* without an in-depth analysis of what constitutes a "parent" or parental unit. We know that Latinxs value extended family members (including grandparents, godparents, and friends with the authority of parents), but is the Latinx notion of "parents" the same as the U.S. construct of as one mother and one father? Other questions arise from the literature, such as the role of specific family members in the education of their children. How might a mother be involved in the education of her children differently than a father? Does gender have an impact on the kinds of messages imparted regarding education? Further, considering that LatCrit and CRT are approaches where storytelling is valued, what are the narratives of children regarding how they experience parental involvement?

In 1970, Latinxs made up 4.7% of the total U.S. population. The most recent Census data show that by 2060, Latinxs will be make up 28.6% of the national population (U.S. Census Bureau, 2018) and if current trends persist, that population will be entering our nation's classrooms, and there is already growth in the numbers of Latinxs enrolled in kindergarten to 12th grade. When Latinxs are projected to be the statistical majority in the United States, is it possible for educational systems to suggest that assimilation is the key to educational equity? How would assimilation be enforced and regulated? How can we reform our U.S. educational system to make accept and affirm the assets that Latinx families bring to the educational landscape? The strand of CRT that calls for action sees such reform not as an opportunity for division, but an opportunity to envision parental engagement anew and along with it, the endless potential for genuine school and parent partnerships that will, in the end, afford all of our nation's children with possibilities yet to be imagined.

Notes

1. When compared to white, middle-class parents.
2. Wellman's (1977) definition of racism as: "culturally sanctioned beliefs which, regardless of the intentions involved, define the advantages Whites have because of the subordinated positions of racial minorities" (p. xviii).
3. The rationale for the use of Chicanx is similar to the rationale for using Latinx.
4. Property functions 1–3 as noted in Dixson & Rousseau, 2006, pp. 22–24.
5. "If one is not born into a family whose knowledge is already deemed valuable, one can then access the knowledge of the middle and upper classes and the potential for social mobility through formal schooling" (Bourdieu & Passeron cited in Yosso, 2005, p. 168).
6. Cultural capital would include education and language; social capital would include one's networks and connections; and economic capital would include monetary resources and valuable assets (Yosso, 2006, p. 174).

References

Antrop-Gonzalez, R., Velez, W., & Garrett, T. (2005). Donde estan los estudiantes Puertorriquenos/os exitosos? [Where are the academically successful Puerto Rican students?]: Success factors of high-achieving Puerto Rican high school students. *Journal of Latinos & Education, 4*(2), 77–94.

Auerbach, S. (2006). "If the student is good, let him fly": Moral support for college among Latino immigrant parents. *Journal of Latinos & Education, 5*(4), 275–292.

Bourdieu, P., & Passeron, J. (1977). *Reproduction in education, society, and culture.* London, UK: Sage.

Crenshaw, K. (2002). The first decade: Critical reflections, or "A foot in the closing door." In F. Valdes, J. McCristal Culp, & A. Harris (Eds.), *Crossroads, directions, and a new critical race theory* (pp. 9–31). Philadelphia, PA: Temple University Press.

Crenshaw, K., Gotanda, N., Peller, G., & Thomas, K. (Eds.). (1995). *Critical race theory: The key writings that formed the movement.* New York, NY: The New Press.

DeCuir, J. T., & Dixson, A. D. (2004). "So when it comes out, they aren't that surprised that it is there": Using critical race theory as a tool of analysis of race and racism in education. *Educational Researcher, 33*(5), 26–31.

Delgado Bernal, D. (1997). *Chicana school resistance and grass roots leadership: Providing an alternative history of the 1968 East Los Angeles blowouts.* Los Angeles, CA: University of California.

Delgado, R. (1988). Critical legal studies and the realities of race: Does the fundamental contradiction have a corollary? *Harvard Civil Rights-Civil Liberties Law Review, 23,* 407–413.

Delgado, R. (1989). Storytelling for oppositionists and others: A plea for narrative. *Michigan Law Review, 87,* 2411–2441.

Delgado, R., & Stefancic, J. (2001). *Critical race theory: An introduction.* New York: New York University Press.

Delgado-Gaitán, C. (1994). *Consejos*: The power of cultural narratives. *Anthropology & Education Quarterly, 25*(3), 298–316.

Delgado-Gaitan, C. (2001). *The power of community: Mobilizing for family and schooling.* Denver, CO: Rowman and Littlefield.

Dixson, A. D., & Rousseau, C. K. (Eds.). (2006). *Critical race theory in education: All God's children got a song.* New York, NY: Routledge.

Elenes, C. A., Gonzalez, F., Delgado Bernal, D., & Villenas, S. (2001). Introduction: Chicana/Mexicana feminist pedagogies: Consejos, respeto, y educacion in everyday life. *International Journal of Qualitative Studies in Education (QSE), 14*(5), 595–602.

Espinoza, L., & Harris, A. (1998). Embracing the tar baby: LatCrit theory and the sticky mess of race. *La Raza Law Journal, 10*(1), 499–559.

Farber, D., & Sherry, S. (1993). Telling stories out of school: An essay on legal narratives. *Stanford Law Review, 45,* 807–854.

Faulstich Orellana, M. (2003). *In other words: En otras palabras: Learning from bilingual kids' translating/interpreting experiences.* Evanston, IL: School of Education and Social Policy, Northwestern University.

Flores, A., G. López, & J. Radford. (2017). Facts on Latinos, 2015. *Pew Research Center.* Retrieved from http://www.pewhispanic.org/2017/09/18/facts-on-u-s-latinos-trend-data/

Freire, P. (1970). *Education for critical consciousness.* New York, NY: Continuum.

Giroux, H. (1983). Theories of reproduction and resistance in the new sociology of education: A critical analysis. *Harvard Educational Review, 53*(3), 257–293.

Hardiman, R., Jackson, B., & Griffin, P. (2010). Conceptual frameworks. In M. Adams, W. J. Blumenfeld, R. Castañeda, H. W. Hackman, M. L. Peters, & X. Zúñiga (Eds.), *Readings for diversity and social justice* (2nd ed., pp. 26–35). New York, NY: Routledge.

Harris, C. (1993). Whiteness as property. *Harvard Law Review, 106,* 1707–1791.

Harro, B. (2008). Updated version of "The cycle of socialization" (2000). In M. Adams, W. J. Blumenfeld, R. Castañeda, H. W. Hackman, M. L. Peters, & X. Zúñiga (Eds.), *Readings for diversity and social justice* (pp. 463–469). New York, NY: Routledge.

hooks, b. (1994). *Teaching to transgress: Education as the practice of freedom.* New York: Routledge.

Kumashiro, K. K. (2000). Toward a theory of anti-oppressive education. *Review of Educational Research, 70*(1), 25–53.

Lopez, G. (2003). Parental involvement as racialized performance. In G. Lopez & L. Parker (Eds.), *Interrogating racism in qualitative research methodology* (pp. 71–95). New York, NY: Peter Lang.

Love, B. (2000). Developing a liberatory consciousness. In M. Adams, W. Blumenfeld, R. Castañeda, H. Hackman, M. Peters, & X. Zúñiga (Eds.), *Readings for diversity and social justice: An anthology on racism, antisemitism, sexism, heterosexism, ableism, and classism* (pp. 470–474). New York, NY: Routledge.

Love, B. (2004). Brown plus 50 counter-storytelling: A critical race theory analysis of the majoritarian achievement gap story. *Equity & Excellence in Education, 37*(3), 227–246.

Matsuda, M. (1991). Voices of America: Accent, antidiscrimination law, and a jurisprudence for the last reconstruction. *Yale Law Journal, 100*(5), 1329–1407.

Merriam-Webster's Collegiate Dictionary (1991). New York, NY: Random House.

McIntosh, P. (1990, Winter). White privilege: Unpacking the invisible knapsack. *Independent School, 31–36.*

National Center for Education Statistics, U.S. Department of Education. (2013). *Indicators of school crime and safety.* Retrieved from https://nces.ed.gov/pubs2013/2013036.pdf

Pharr, S. (1995). Homophobia a weapon of sexism. In P. Rothenberg (Ed.), *Race, class and gender in the United States: An integrated study* (pp. 475–490). New York, NY: St. Martin's Press.

Plessy v. Ferguson. (1896). 163 US 537.

Posner, R. A. (1995). *Overcoming law.* Cambridge, MA: Harvard University Press.

Reese, L. J. (1992). *Ecocultural factors influencing the academic success of young Latino students.* Los Angeles, CA: University of California.

Regents of University of California v. Bakke. (1978). 438 US 265.

Solórzano, D., & Delgado Bernal, D. (2001). Critical race theory, transformational resistance, and social justice: Chicana and Chicano students in an urban context. *Urban Education, 36*(3), 308–342.

Solórzano, D. G., & Yosso, T. J. (2001). From racial stereotyping and deficit discourse toward a critical race theory in teacher education. *Multicultural Education, 9*(1), 2–8.

Stanton-Salazar, R. D. (2001). *Manufacturing hope and despair: The school and kin support networks of capital U.S.-Mexican youth.* New York, NY: Teachers College Press.

Tatum, B. D. (2017). *Why are all the black kids sitting together in the cafeteria? And other conversations about race.* (3rd ed.). New York, NY: Basic Books.

Tushnet, M. (1992). The degradation of constitutional discourse. *Georgetown Law Review, 81,* 1151–1193.

U.S. Census Bureau. (2018). *Hispanic Heritage Month 2018.* Retrieved from https://www.census.gov/newsroom/facts-for-features/2018/hispanic-heritage-month.html

Wildman, S., & Davis, A. (2000). Language and silence: Making systems of privilege visible. In M. Adams, W. Blumenfeld, R. Castañeda, H. Hackman, M. Peters, & X. Zúñiga (Eds.), *Readings for diversity and social justice: An anthology on racism, antisemitism, sexism, heterosexism, ableism, and classism.* New York, NY: Routledge.

Yosso, T. J. (2006). Whose culture has capital? A critical race theory discussion of community cultural wealth. In A. Dixson & C. Rousseau (Eds.), *Critical race theory in education: All God's children got a song.* New York, NY: Routledge.

MANIFESTATIONS OF CULTURAL CAPITAL

Participants at Smith College

Smith College is a highly selective, liberal arts, PWI located in a small town in Western Massachusetts. The college is relatively small with about 2,500 undergraduate students enrolled. Founded in 1871, the mission of the college is to empower women and prepare them for "lives of distinction." Sophia Smith, the college's founder had expressed an intention of having the college located in the center of a town, so the students could be a part of the life of the town and so the town could be a part of the institution. Northampton, the town that the college is located in could be described as the "idyllic" college town, offering many coffee shops, novelty stores, restaurants, and pubs. While a female President presently leads the college, it wasn't until 1975 that the institution was led by its first female President, Jill Ker Conway. Most of the students enrolled at the college live within a house system on campus in dwellings that more closely resemble cottages. Not all of the undergraduate students enrolled are "traditionally aged" students, with non-traditional aged students enrolled at the college in the Ada Comstock Scholars program.

While the college offers an array of courses in the arts and humanities, it has received attention for its science program, the renown of being a gender inclusive institution with an engineering program, and a large endowment. This attention to engineering was due to the leadership of the college's ninth

President, Ruth J. Simmons, the first African-American woman to lead an institution with this profile. Although the college is an institution that reports graduating female undergraduate students, there is a population of female to male (FTM), non-binary, and gender non-conforming (GNC) identified students enrolled. Students come from all of the six populated continents. Despite the college's stated commitment and desire to create a diverse learning community, only 10% identify as Latinx. The demographic summary is provided below (Table 5.1).

Table 5.1: Smith College Common Data Set, 2017–2018.

Racial/Cultural Categories	Degree-Seeking Undergraduates (includes first-time first-year)
Nonresident aliens	349
Hispanic	260
Black or African American, non-Hispanic	166
White, non-Hispanic	1,197
American Indian or Alaska Native, non-Hispanic	3
Asian, non-Hispanic	275
Native Hawaiian or other Pacific Islander, non-Hispanic	3
Two or more races, non-Hispanic	110
Race and/or ethnicity unknown	156
Total	**2,521**

Source: Author.

Data Collection

Students, staff, and the Faculty Advisor to the Latina student organization were contacted at to recruit participants. This was done by sending the "Call for Participants Letter" via email. Participants who were interested in being a part of this research study were then to complete a "Demographic Questionnaire" to determine their eligibility to participate in the study. Once participants were deemed eligible, they were forwarded a copy of the "Informed Consent Form" and asked to bring a signed copy with them to our first meeting. These meetings were established through email communication. At the first meeting, participants were given a signed copy of the Informed Consent Form and were invited to ask any questions about me, the nature of the study, and where they could direct questions. After discussing their participant rights an in-depth interview was scheduled. Participants were notified that they would be asked to complete an online Likert Scale survey prior to the interview and that they would be invited to participate in a focus group meeting. My call for participants was forwarded to the President of the Latina cultural organization who then forwarded it on to her group, *Nosotras*. She consented to an in-depth interview, so she could become familiar with the nature of the study. After having done so, she sought permission from the group to have me attend a "general body" meeting, where there would be a greater number of students in attendance (which differs from their Executive Board meetings that have a smaller number of attendants) where I conducted a focus group and recruited interview participants. A traditional Puerto Rican dinner of *pernil* (pork) and *arroz con gandules* (rice and pigeon peas) was offered to ensure that participants would not miss dinnertime because of attendance at the focus group. Additionally, I wanted something that would make the participants feel at "home" and the homemade meal was a big draw.

There were 18 Latina students in attendance at the focus group that was held in the multicultural space at the college. Of the 18 students in attendance, 11 volunteered to take part in a 90–120 minute individual semi-structured interviews. All 11 participants provided complete data sets.[1] Between the focus group attendees and in-depth interviews, a total of 18 students participated in the study. Focus group questions were used to guide the discussion. The focus group themes that emerged were consistent with the themes of the in-depth interviews, and facilitating a focus group was helpful as students who were apprehensive to speak in the individual interviews spoke more freely in a larger group. Additionally, focus groups help participants to build off of other ideas and responses generated from the group.

Description and Interpretation of Parental Engagement

During focus groups and in-depth interviews, participants were asked about how their parents were involved and engaged in their early education. I provided no definition or history of involvement, as I felt that such information would be leading and might interfere with the data. Students would describe parents as being "strict," meaning that there were clear expectations and explicit consequences for failing to meet those expectations. One participant shared that her mother started a childcare business in their home so she could monitor the activities and school attendance of her daughter. Another participant shared that her mother was involved through the parental practice of monitoring (Antrop-González, Velez, & Garrett, 2005; Arzubiaga, Ceja, & Artiles, 2000). When asked, "What was report card day like at home?" this participant shared:

> She knew we had a report card. If we didn't give it to her, she would look through your book bag and be like, "Oh, where's your report card? Oh it doesn't matter if you don't bring it. I'm going to your school to get it anyway."

The theme of monitoring was raised by another participant who said that her mother would come home from work and check her homework and book bag and emphasized checking for a tidy book bag as a demonstration of engagement.

One participant spoke of how there was a clear routine and expectation regarding the completion of homework and shared that her mother would "sit with us and make us do our homework, and we couldn't get up until we were finished." Another demonstration of parental engagement was evidenced through the time spent with students on homework and school issues. Taking the time to invest in their education, despite a busy and complicated work schedule, was something that the participants noted. "They took the time to check my homework" or "Dad would take time to drive me to school" showed participants that school was a priority and something their parents took very seriously.

Parental engagement was also shown through parents showing up at school to talk to a teacher about unfair or inaccurate grading practices. One participant's father had gone to his daughter's school because she was upset about a grade she received on a math test. The father showed the math teacher that she had made erroneous calculations and issued the wrong grade. Another participant's mother challenged her daughter's English teacher because she "never gave anything higher than an 85."

In contrast to how their parents were engaged in their early education, participants were asked how they felt their parents were engaged in their college education. Participants in the study were quick to name the fact that parental engagement had changed because their parents were unfamiliar with the college experience. They may have had a child go to college, but the experience of having a child leave the state to attend school was a foreign idea for some. Where parents had been involved with trips to a child's classroom teacher, this was no longer possible because of college norms that called for students to be self-advocates in their education. While they had once helped with middle-school level math, parents were not prepared to assist with statistics. Nonetheless, parents still offered moral and emotional support and demonstrated involvement and investment in the education of their children through that support.

This investment started as early as move-in day for some participants. When asked, "Who moved you to Smith?" participants would roll their eyes and respond, "The whole family!" When I probed for clarity on what was meant by the "whole family," I was given the list of aunts, uncles, grandparents, cousins, parents, and family friends who had made the trip to see where the student would be spending the next four years and to help her settle in to her new room. I asked, "What did everyone do when they arrived at your room?" and was given a list of chores that various members performed, such as cleaning the room, making the bed, hanging up the clothes, affixing a crucifix over the bed, unpacking suitcases, and mopping the floors with Pine Sol or Mistolín, which are household cleaning products preferred by some Latinx families. Although the roles were gender specific, men would take on the tasks of hanging hooks and setting up electronic devices and women would get to the tasks of beautifying the room. I asked participants, "Why do you think they did all of those things?" and the responses revealed that their families wanted to give them "a sense of home."

Prior to returning home for a college break, students reported that their mothers would ask ¿Que quieres comer? (What would you like to eat?) and upon arriving home would be fed their requested meals and find that their parents had purchased their favorite foods for them to enjoy during their stay. In a sense, food is cultural capital, a reward, motivator, and comfort in Latinx households. The college's dining halls serve "traditional fare," such as pastas, sandwiches, salads, and various meat products. When Smith College and as other colleges attempt to be inclusive of other cultures with a "themed" dinner, these dinners are reported to be lacking the flavor of home. One student shared in a focus group, "It's been a long time since I had some good rice!" Going home to enjoy a meal that is reserved for special occasions has been reported as a highlight of returning home. One participant from California spoke about the planning that is done over the phone prior to her return home

We talk every day. If I don't call them at a certain time, they're like "Are you ok? Just send me a text." Or they'll send notes in the mail from time to time or when I go home it's like, "Oh, what do you want? What would you like to eat? Where would you like to go? Should we go out to Disneyland?" and I'm like, "Mom, I still live here, it's not like I am a visitor." But they just feel that they want me to feel comfort while I have that little time when I am at home, and that's their way of showing that they care.

Parents also offered messages about self-care, and these were the same at home as when students were away at college. Students were reminded to eat, sleep, and relax.

While students appreciated the ways in which their parents were involved, they also voiced frustration that their parents couldn't be as involved as "other" parents[2] in their college education. This was through no fault of the parents but due to a lack of access to social capital provided through a formal education. One participant offered the following:

> Now that I have graduation coming up and I'm graduating, they're like, "I don't understand why graduation is like a whole weekend like why do we have to go up there?" And I'm like, "I didn't come up with that. I didn't apply here thinking that. I'm sorry" and I'm like, "Damn, shouldn't you just be happy that I'm graduating from someplace?"

One student felt that she was receiving negative attention from her family when she returned for January Term, which at Smith College, similar to other colleges, lasts for one month. She was being questioned by her family for being able to be away from college when her cousins in college didn't have such a break. She felt as if she was being accused of having dropped out of school and trying to hide it. While she felt that this was a demonstration of a lack of appreciation of her accomplishment of going to school out of state, I felt this comment and the comment regarding the duration of Commencement activities was more reflective of lack of access to social capital. Some families may have no prior knowledge that winter break can last a month at some institutions, and some families may be unfamiliar with the word "interterm" altogether if they do not have the access to varied college experiences and practices.

When parents have completed a college education in their country of origin, students are able to explain college-level concepts in a familiar area of study and even then a sense of distance is created.

> My dad graduated. He has a master's in his country, and it's very different. In high school, he was able to help me because he was at my level that he could still help me but now that I'm in college, it's a little bit different because I'll call him and say, "Hey, let's discuss what I learned in my sports econ class" and he feels intimidated because he knows I'm getting to know more than he does now.

Some parents reverted to familiar support tactics when they didn't know how to offer the support that students were seeking. One such practice was to push students to earn good grades. Participants reported being frustrated with this because they felt that their parents didn't understand that an "A" or a "B+" meant something different in college than it did in high school.

Regardless of distance or misunderstanding, Latinx parents make endless attempts to be involved through demonstrations of support. Parents, whether they could afford it or not, would send college advertised care packages and attend Family Weekend at the college. When I asked why the family would make this sacrifice, students told me that parents didn't want their children to feel alone. There seemed to be an unspoken fear harbored by the parents that their children would feel unsupported as other students received packages and spent the weekend with their families. The practice of ensuring that students didn't feel alone took place during regular phone calls with participants. During these conversations, parents would remind their children that they were capable of completing their college educations. One father sent a letter to his daughter that said "I'm so proud of you. You're an inspiration to me." Parents also told participants how they had been boasting to their bosses or co-workers about their daughter "who is a college student!" If they weren't told this directly, extended family would call saying that they had heard about the participant's good grades from their parents or told "they are always talking about you." Calls from home also contain messages like "We'll be proud of you as long as you do your best" and parents provided reminders of all of the other life challenges students were able to surmount. One participant reported that she felt better after having revisited life obstacles and was surprised that her father could remember so many and in such detail.

Employing Cultural Messages Regarding Education

In order to understand how Latinx college students are employing cultural messages through what their parents imparted about education, it is important to learn what those messages were. The data collected and analyzed in this research study is consistent with the literature that supports Latinxs are invested in education (Delgado-Gaitán, 1994; Moles et al., 1993; Trueba & Delgado-Gaitán, 1988). Similarly, parents of college students spoke of the importance of education in the lives of their children. One participant spoke of how her mother shared messages about the necessity of completing an education. She emphasized the seriousness of her message by completing her own course of study to become a nurse.

> She never quit going to school, regardless if she had to take care of me, got to work, and got [*sic*] to school. No matter how long it took to finish, she wanted me to know that no matter what, you have to finish your education. You didn't have to be rich and fabulous just live a good and ordinary life. You didn't have to struggle to get the basic necessities.

There were parents who lamented about their own unrealized dreams of pursuing a college degree as participants shared the following with me:

> But to this day she always says that she wishes she could have gone to school, and she says that she came to this country so we could have a better future and that we needed to go to school and college. It's kind of like she always said she wanted us to do what she wasn't able to do.

A participant who was the first high school graduate in her family shared:

> I know for her it was just important that I finish high school because she never got to do it. My grandmother never did it. Back in those days in Puerto Rico, there was no high school really for women.

Another participant shared that her father started college "but couldn't finish due to family issues" and that both parents imparted that "education was good for you. It could open doors for you, and you could do something with your life."

Participants also shared that their parents demonstrated a value for education through the personal sacrifices they were willing to make solely for the purpose of obtaining a good education for their children in the United States. One participant poignantly stated:

> My mother had a life in Ecuador. My mother was a rich girl. She had maids. She had everybody and my father did what he had to do. They had a life, and they had an amazing life, and for them to come here and all of a sudden to go back to zero, like they lost their education. My father was a lawyer, and he came back here, and he had to end up working in a factory and do things he's never done in his life. For him to do that is the reason why I did do well in high school is the reason why my mother did sit with up and wait with me to finish my homework. She was there if I had to go to school, and I was a little late. She didn't care what was going on, she would take me. She didn't have a car but the *vecino* (neighbor) knew somebody who knew somebody, and I would get there no matter what, thanks to my parents. And for me, I'm the immigrant story. My parents are immigrants. They're here to give us a better life. I have an older brother. He graduated, and he did his part because he finished. He

did school, and he's still going, and for me, it's like I have to finish this and it's hard for my parents to have me here...The only reason I'm here is for them and to prove and just to fulfill the goal of all the suffering for all these things of why they had to go through everything just for me to do it and the second, I'm at your [researcher's] level and when I'm graduating [participant pauses to cry] I'll feel so good because it's the reason for why my parents did it, and why your parents go through all that because they want to see you fulfilled and when I'm there, I want to be really good, and I did it for them. I did it for my brother, and I did it for myself.

Students employ the cultural message that education is important by pledging to, and eventually succeeding in the act of accomplishing their goals of "finishing" school. The concept of "finishing" will be discussed further in chapter nine.

Lessons on the importance of education would not be the only lesson that parents would impart to their children. Parents would also send their children off with cultural capital to prepare their children for hostile conditions. These would come in the form of the six forms of cultural capital (aspirational, familial, linguistic, navigational, resistance, social). This research study set out to examine how those forms of capital were being utilized.

Manifestations of Cultural Capital

Aspirational Capital. Parents transmit aspirational capital by encouraging children to hold on to their hopes and dreams despite obstacles. Latinx students at Smith College utilized that capital to push themselves beyond the limits of what they thought was possible for themselves or what had been achieved in their families. One participant connected the goal of completing her college education to her identity as a woman:

I just feel like everybody gives credit to the men in the group. My cousins, two of them are cops, the other one is a Marine, and they're so successful, and the women in the family just so fill the stereotype. Like one of my cousins got pregnant at a young age, and the other didn't go to college. I'm going to be the first woman to graduate college in the U.S., and it feels really good and honestly, I'm doing it for my mom because she showed me that women can do it, too. That's why I'm doing it, to show them that women can make them proud.

When participants were asked, "What is keeping you in college?" they talked about wanting to complete their college educations, and they talked about the hopes and dreams that they have for the future. This participant shared:

> I just want to make sure that I'm going to be able to take care of them [parents]. Also my small sister, my younger sister, I want to be an example for her, and I want her to do well in school and go to college. It's also for me because I want to be someone in life, and I want to make sure that I'm going to be able to be dependent when I grow up. And if I someday decide to have children, they're not going to be suffering because of me or because they don't have money or they don't have the resources. They have a parent who wants to help them.

Students who were sophomores and juniors were already considering post-baccalaureate programs and planning ahead for what they would need to do to meet admissions requirements at those programs.

Familial Capital. As discussed in chapter one, parents impart familial capital through members of the family and extended family. These individuals model important cultural values, such as education, and lessons communicated by family enlighten a student's awareness on emotional and moral levels.

Students demonstrate a utilization of this capital in the way in which they replicate familial structures. The importance of *Nosotras* is one such example. While participants are quick to explain that the organization is not actually family but like a family, the hierarchy of the organization is set up very much like a nuclear or single household family. The year that the study was conducted, there was one president of the organization. She was a senior who consulted with the group but who was the ultimate spokesperson for the group. In the past, there have been organizational co-chairs who, would consult with the group but would ultimately make final decisions and be the representatives for the group. The organization even assigns siblings to new students and members of the group. You can get a sibling in the group even if at home, you are an only child. Similar to the finding that there is a positive rivalry that exists among actual siblings and family members, the students in this organization also look to fellow high achieving members as role models and people to "keep up with."

An interesting observation of this group has been that in their replication of family structure, they also replicate the ways in which the six forms of capital are passed down. Aspirational, linguistic, navigational, resistance, and social capital are all transmitted throughout the group. One student explained the rationale behind "creating culture" when she explained:

> It's a lot harder for us because there are not a lot of us and not that we have to assimilate, but we have to get used to a culture that's not our own. So Latinas have to make our own culture, make this college what we know because we have to survive because this is not what we know.

Of note is the fact that what these students chose as a survival mechanism and one that is culturally recognizable is that of family.

Linguistic Capital. Linguistic capital is related to the tradition of storytelling. This kind of storytelling can include *consejos* (advice) or *refranes* (proverb-style messages) and demonstrates linguistic strengths in the ability to tell a story while employing comedic timing, intonation, memorization, facial expressions, and dramatic pauses. I was able to witness this capital in action when I observed participants during the focus group and when members of the organization recognized one another on campus. While the exchanges were brief, participants told stories about other students, going so far as to re-enact the story they had been a part of. During in-depth interviews, some participants told stories that they had heard that were so convincing, they seemed to be a part of the participants' own memories and experiences. The most memorable of these stories was when a participant shared the story of a Latina mother who attended a function for newly admitted Smith College students.

> One of the *Nosotras* girls said the first time—the only time—her mom went to one of those meetings, because it's in the home of an SWC alum, that she got so excited when she saw another Hispanic lady. She was like, "OH HI!" And she wanted to talk, and then she noticed that she was the maid, and she was like, "Oh, never mind."

Storytelling and shared memories seems to reinforce the familial connection that these women have created amongst themselves.

Navigational Capital. Children who receive this capital are fortified with inner resources and resilience that empowers them to endure stressful events and hostile environments. This capital was manifested among Latinas at the college who felt a personal obligation to support and encourage and empower fellow Latina students who were questioning their right to be a student at the college. They described what it was like to be Latina on campus and how they coped with their feelings of being in a space where they found themselves to be members of a statistical minority. One participant described the experience of having to reassure an incoming first-year student of her uniqueness and her ability to be seen as an individual:

> Let's say it's your first class, and you're standing around the class. You're going to be one of the only people of color and one of the only people where your parents are like immigrants. And I shouldn't think of it like that because everybody's an immigrant, so like everybody's Hispanic, so she [the first year student] doesn't really see that. It's like making her unique among the other girls, I guess.

Another woman talked about how she gained support and perspective from fellow Latinas and students of color when she noticed feeling intimidated by being at a PWI:

> I remember when I did the program Bridges,[3] and I was talking to one of my Bridges leaders, and I was like, "I'm a little intimidated. I'm going to be honest because you know I come from a completely different background than most of the women here," and she was like, "Don't worry about it when you go to the classroom. You go and you act like you own it. Not raise your hand for every question, but you contribute and that shows that even though you're here and you're not of the same class or whatever the case may be, but at the same time you have the knowledge, and you didn't have the same resources to get here, but you still made it."

Participants felt that imparting these messages to students who were struggling with the lack of diversity on campus or doubtful of their abilities was key in ensuring that these students were successful and remained enrolled at this college.

Resistance Capital. This capital is of particular use at a setting such as Smith College, a predominantly White institution that was designed without people of color in mind.[4] Resistance capital teaches students how to employ oppositional behavior to challenge inequality.

Utilization of this capital was evidenced in two ways. First, it was evidenced through a sophisticated student critique of the inequality in operation at Smith. One student concluded:

> I think one of the biggest problems at Smith is that the school still operates as if it were a white, middle-class institution. I feel that they just ignore us minorities in the sense that they don't take into account the things that we need in order to succeed, and they won't do anything to bridge the gap between us and the majority of the students here.

An analysis such as this is oppositional in itself in that white privilege and social constructions are not considered to be topics for "polite conversation" at Smith College and are therefore not discussed. As one participant questioned, "Why don't we focus on students of color?"

Another way in which this capital manifests is when students speak up to educate others in the classroom. One participant described the rationale behind her utilization of this capital in the classroom setting and what she feels she stands to lose if she doesn't employ resistance capital when she shared the following:

I feel that the minute you forget where you come from, you lose everything. You lose yourself, you lose your values. And I feel like that's when your life starts going out of control, when you forget the things that are important to you. And I feel like that happens very often, being at a place like this. It's very easy to assimilate into the mainstream and not stand up for the things you value, the things that make you who you are because it's easier. In my classes I'm known as the crazy Puerto Rican,[5] and I've gotten passionate about the human rights violations of Puerto Ricans by the American government. So any opportunity I have to bring that up, I do. What if I didn't bring that up? I'm going to be suppressing that voice inside of me. When you start doing that, you start losing yourself.

This is directly linked to what this participant learned from her mother. During the focus group, I asked participants to share what messages they had carried with them from their parents to Smith. After one participant shared, "Don't forget where you came from," this participant contributed, "My mom always tells me, 'just remember the things in your life that have made you who you are because without those experiences, you wouldn't be who you are today.'" Remembering who she is and the self-obligation to be true to oneself is what compels these students to speak out against injustice.

Social Capital. Parents who transmitted social capital to their children also transmitted the skill of utilizing social networks to obtain resources needed for their children to experience positive educational outcomes. Similarly, within a self-created family, the members of *Nosotras* were able to utilize social networks for themselves and fellow women of color when they exercise social capital.

One student talked about needing to find a way to get herself and her sister (also a Smith College student) a way to get to their grandmother's funeral in California. The participant asked a peer she thought might offer some guidance and that networking was met with positive results. The participant asked her friend for potential resources during lunchtime and by dinnertime, her friend had a list of college resources that she could email and provided advice on what to say in the email. The participant and her sister followed this advice and were both able to be with their families in California for a funeral service later that week.

Another participant described how she felt the college had deprived students of color of available resources (book, internship, and junior year abroad funding) by not being transparent in advertising these opportunities. When describing how she learned about resources at the college, the student disclosed, "The only reason I found out is because another woman of color told me. Other than that, if you're not speaking to people of color who are finding out about information, you're not going to get the information." This student felt that for her, if she wanted access to resources, she would need to use her network of women of color, a source of social capital she did have access to.

Students at Smith were able to describe and interpret parental engagement during their early education as being a very "hands-on" process and described how parental engagement was based more on moral support during their current college experiences. Participants were also able to describe parental messages regarding the importance of education. Parental stories of personal struggle and sacrifice endured to secure a good education for their children inspired participants to "finish" school and fulfill the dreams that their parents held on to. Participants at Smith manifested all six forms of capital mainly through the replication of the Latinx family culture.

The accounts of the Smith College participants particularly resonated with me perhaps because I am also a Latinx graduate of the same college. I clearly recall move-in day at the college and my Mom, sister, aunt, uncle and grandfather riding in the van. My uncle had made a wooden trailer and engineered it with working taillights. I didn't need the trailer because I had so many belongings; we had the trailer because I had so much *familia*. I was a passenger in a different car that held my plants and my 90's-era stereo system. The familial tasks the participants talked about mirrored my own experience and a similar narrative is found in the work of Capó Crucet (2015). My uncle went about the business of setting up my stereo while my Mom and aunt cleaned despite my protests that the housekeeping staff had already cleaned. My Mother made it clear that the room wasn't clean because *she* hadn't cleaned it. While my Mother wouldn't be able to give me advice pertinent to my first days of college, she could make my room feel like a home away from home, and in so doing, was creating a mental health space and demonstrating engagement. When my family left, and I would not find this out until the end of the spring semester, the women on the same floor of the house referred to me as "the thing" because they couldn't understand the number of people who had moved me in, and I would spend my first semester without friends in my house. The transference of familial capital inspired me to seek out surrogate siblings and was my means of survival in that difficult first semester. Had the college residential life staff been versed in the cultural way that my family was showing up to support me, perhaps that first semester would have been different.

Notes

1. A complete data set included a demographic questionnaire, Likert-scale, and interview.
2. These were revealed to be white parents with college degrees.
3. Name for a pre-orientation program at the college for women of color designed to familiarize them with campus resources prior to the official start of the academic year.
4. In the literature, this particular design that marginalizes people of color is regarded as a "hostile environment."
5. This participant self-identified as Dominican.

References

Antrop-Gonzalez, R., Velez, W., & Garrett, T. (2005). Donde estan los estudiantes Puertorriquenos/os exitosos? [Where are the academically successful Puerto Rican students?]: Success factors of high-achieving Puerto Rican high school students. *Journal of Latinos & Education, 4*(2), 77–94.

Arzubiaga, A., Ceja, M., & Artiles, A. (2000). Transcending deficit thinking about latinos' parenting styles: Toward an ecocultural view of family life. In C. Martinez, Z. Leonardo, & C. Tejeda (Eds.), *Charting new terrains of Chicana(o)/Latina(o) education* (pp. 93–106). Cresskill, NJ: Hampton Press.

Capó Crucet, J. (2015, August 22). *Taking my parents to college.* Retrieved from https://www.nytimes.com/2015/08/23/opinion/sunday/taking-my-parents-to-college.html?partner=rssnyt&emc=rss

Delgado-Gaitán, C. (1994). Consejos: The power of cultural narratives. *Anthropology & Education Quarterly, 25*(3), 298–316.

Moles, O., D'Angelo, D., & Office of Educational Research and Improvement (ED). (1993). *Building school-family partnerships for learning: Workshops for urban educators.* (ERIC Document Reproduction Service No. ED364651).

Trueba, H., & Delgado-Gaitán, C. (1988). *Minority achievement and parental support: Academic resocialization through mentoring.* Santa Barbara, CA: University of California.

· 6 ·

MANIFESTATIONS OF CULTURAL CAPITAL

Participants at the University of Massachusetts at Amherst

The University of Massachusetts (UMASS) at Amherst campus is part of the state's University system, which consists of five universities and has approximately 24,000 students. This would make the student population 10 times bigger than Smith College. UMASS is situated in the small town of Amherst, and former home to Emily Dickinson that offers coffee shops, restaurants, bars, bookstores, and a small movie theater. The university was founded in 1863 originally intended to be a land-grant agricultural college. At its inception, the curriculum included liberal arts, farming, science, and technical courses. There were four faculty members and 56 students enrolled.

In 1892 UMASS admitted its first female student and graduate degrees were instated. In 1947 it went from being a college to becoming a University and this change was reflected in the broader curriculum, facilities, and larger student population. The UMASS student population seemed to reflect the political climate of the United States. After World War II with veterans returning home, there was a growth in enrollment and a growth in the facilities to support the 4,000 students enrolled there in 1954. In the 1960s as "Baby Boomers" were able to enroll in the university, enrollment grew to 10,500. UMASS students would initiate a protest of the political climate of the day that resulted in a takeover of the main administration building. By the end of the 1960s UMASS saw the building of a new residential area and new academic departments that reflect what the university looks like today.

The 1970s brought additional changes. A completion of the college library in 1973 earned UMASS the distinction of having the tallest library in the world, and the university also added a parking garage, restaurant, campus center, hotel, and fine arts center. The 1970s to the 1990s would earn UMASS the distinction in the areas of sports and research with a basketball championship and new graduate research center.

Within the geographical area in which the university is situated, it has gained a reputation for being a "party school," an image that they are constantly trying to change and one that some students seem to resent. Despite this image, it is seen by the local community as a good school with a serious academic program. Demographically, women outnumber men both in undergraduate and graduate enrollment numbers. There are on-campus resources for men, women, LGBT students, international students, honors students, and students with disabilities, to name a few. Students come from all over the United States and all over the world to attend UMASS. Participants in the study were residents of Massachusetts and, therefore, were within driving distance to their families, although they did not reside with their families, and 6% of Latinx students make up the student body. A demographic summary[1] can be found below (Table 6.1.).

Table 6.1: UMASS Amherst Common Data Set, 2017–2018.

Racial/Cultural Categories	Degree-Seeking Undergraduates (includes first-time first-year)
Nonresident aliens	1,376
Hispanic	1,466
Black or African American, non-Hispanic	1,007
White, non-Hispanic	14,824
American Indian or Alaska Native, non-Hispanic	26
Asian, non-Hispanic	2,306
Native Hawaiian or other Pacific Islander, non-Hispanic	13
Two or more races, non-Hispanic	643
Race and/or ethnicity unknown	1,349
Total	**23,010**

Source: Author.

Data Collection

Individual students, staff, faculty, and student organization leaders were contacted at UMASS to recruit participants. Similar to what was done at Smith College, a "Call for Participants" email was sent out, respondents were asked to complete the "Demographic Questionnaire," and those who were deemed eligible to continue in the process were forwarded an "Informed Consent Form." A meeting was scheduled where participants were given a copy of the consent form, asked questions about the nature of the study, were told who they could contact about the study, and were informed of their rights as a participant. Participants were notified about the Likert-scale survey, and they were invited to take part in the focus group discussion.

The main contact and my liaison to the students I was working with was an undergraduate UMASS senior with ties to all of the Latinx organizations on campus. He forwarded my "Call for Participants" and spread news of the study through word of mouth. He was the first subject to take part in an in-depth semi-structured interview, and agreed to seek out potential candidates for the study and have them contact me. In the interim between the time of his in-depth interview and the focus group, scheduled interviews were taking place through connections made by staff and faculty. I was invited to hold a focus group in the office of one of the Latinx organizations on campus where I recruited participants. As I had done at Smith College, I provided dinner. Students told me that wings and pizza would be a good way to recruit participants and I provided a meal consisting of those items.

A total of six Latinx students attended the focus group. Of that number, one had already taken part in an in-depth semi-structured interview, and one volunteered to take part in interview but did not respond to my emails. After trying to contact her several times, I ceased my efforts and continued holding interviews with students on my participant list. Ten students made contact with me to take part in interviews; three did not respond to additional email reminders; and seven followed through with the process and completed data sets. The total number of participants between the focus group and in-depth interviews was 11. The focus group themes that emerged were consistent with the themes of the in-depth interviews. Male participants were difficult to recruit, and when there were male participants in the interviews, they did not speak as much as female participants. I can only hypothesize the reasons for this, as I did not make any concerted effort to recruit more women than men. It could be that as I am a female-bodied person that women felt more at ease speaking to me. It could also be that I was asking questions that required self-reflection and a level of vulnerability that sexism excludes men from. The lack of adequate representation of men is a limitation of this research.

Description of Parental Engagement

Similar to the descriptions offered by participants at Smith, parental engagement during early education was reported by UMASS students to be very "hands-on." Participants described having a routine to follow upon returning home from school and that parents would help with homework. During early education there was a strict regimen where schoolwork was concerned. One participant stated, "There was no TV until homework was done, and there was no other option. My family was big on grades, and there was no understanding of bad grades because you didn't like the subject."

Another participant shared:

> Mostly it was, "All right, come and eat first," and then it was, "Just do your homework," basically. My mom always tried to help us. Eventually it came to a point when she couldn't help us, but she was always involved and because of my brother [who is disabled], she was pretty involved in the school system. She knows the school system very well. Always going to meetings, always talking to janitors.

She was not the only participant who would respond that parents would help where they could with school work, but their ability to help was affected by the level of schooling they attained, and as one participant stated, "My mom was able to help with math early on because math is universal."

As was the case with Smith College participants reminiscing about their move-in day, participants also revealed that the type of support and engagement provided was specific to gendered roles. One participant said that her mother was more nurturing when she had difficulty with schoolwork whereas her father, in his attempt to be supportive would say things like, "Man up or shut up."

Parental engagement was also demonstrated in how good grades were rewarded and how bad grades received negative attention and consequences. One participant said that she was paid in cash for good grades, but she would also have to pay her parents back in cash for every bad grade that she earned. When one student got poor marks for conduct and was told that she was "too social" in school, her mother would make her write, "I will not talk in class" 100 times and then hand that in to her teacher. This seemed to be her mother's way of demonstrating to the teacher that she was supportive of what the teacher was doing in the classroom by having her daughter complete the punishment for talking in class.

In contrast to how their parents were involved in their early education, students at the university were asked how their parents are currently involved in their college education. For the most part, participants felt that their parents were okay with them going away to college and admitted that "everyone gets homesick at first." While students at UMASS reported what students at Smith College did—that parents are involved in college but the involvement takes on a different appearance—students in both participant pools described how parents still wanted to ensure that their children were taking care of their basic needs. One participant gave the following example:

> It's always like, "Just do your best," "You know you can do it," "Make sure you eat," "Make sure you're sleeping enough," "Don't stay up too late," just little tips. It makes my day because I know they're trying. You know, "Don't stay out too late," "How's school going?"

Mirroring what was reported regarding move-in day at Smith College, UMASS students shared that their parents and families were also excited and supportive about the move into a college dorm. When I asked one participant, "Who moved you to UMASS?" she laughed and replied, "Everybody!" and then listed that her entourage that day consisted of her "mother, brother, cousin, her husband, his friends, my friends, and one of my aunts." When I asked her what they did when they arrived at her room, she reported:

> They helped me set up my room. They help me put my fridge and all of the food from home. They put it in there. They made my bed. They set up my posters. That was a really sad day. I cried that day. I was like, "What do I do now?"

When asked "why did they help you unpack?" She said replied, "I guess they wanted to make sure that I was okay. There was no one that I really knew out here. They just wanted to know that I was okay. It was just family being family, I guess."

A lack of familiarity with the opening of the academic year was something that first-generation families experienced. One student recalled:

> My parents weren't really there for the high school to college process. They didn't know how to help me. I mean that's understandable but they were just like, "Oh, she's going to college now," but we didn't know once we came here and saw that everybody was moving in. My mom kind of freaked out. Like, "Was I supposed to

bring you food or something or was I supposed to bring snacks? Do you need money? What do we give you?"

Smith College participants and UMASS participants reported that they were greeted with a hero's welcome when they arrived home for a school break. Participants were asked, "What do you want to eat when you're home?" and when participants returned home, they found that their parents had purchased all of their favorite foods. One male student reported:

I get spoiled when I go home. My mom does my laundry and she does too much for me. It's like I want it to stop but I don't want it to stop. I know she misses me, and this is her way of showing me, and I don't want to say, "Stop," and be rude.

Another student said:

I remember waking up during Christmas break to my mom frying food for me during breakfast and my mom was like, "This is for you to take back to school." And I was like, "What time did you get up?" and she would say, "Oh, 8 o'clock in the morning," and there would be all of these Tupperware filled with rice.

When I asked students to theorize on their parents' behavior and why they thought that their parents were going out of their way to welcome their children home, one student said that, "I feel like Spanish parents are more attached to their children. I don't know if attached is the right word."

At this point, another participant chimed in on the close nature of Latinx families: I feel that they just tend to be closer and especially when people tend to go away for a long time, and they've always been there in the house forever, and then they go away for some time or move out, when they do come by, it's like, "Oh my God, you're here! What do you want?!"

Participants reported coming home to find that the rooms that they left have been cleaned and have presents waiting inside for them. These presents usually consist of items to make their college rooms more comfortable and reminiscent of home.

Phone calls to and from home ranged in frequency from three times a day to every two weeks. There didn't seem to be a pattern or profile to who called home, how often, and when. The only distinction was according to gender. Males called home less frequently than women did and were expected to. Despite the length or frequency of contact, one thing was clear. Parents were proud of their children and would boast to their friends and co-workers about having a son or daughter in college. Participants talked about how parents wanted to advertise to the world that they were parents of a UMASS student by sporting UMASS "mom" and "dad" apparel and asking for UMASS "mom" or "dad" sweatshirts, t-shirts, and hats for birthday and holiday presents. One participant said that his dad was sporting a UMASS hat that he bought for himself and as another participant stated, "My parents want UMASS para.²"

Employing Cultural Messages Regarding Education

The messages imparted to UMASS students echoed the sentiments of Smith College parents with the message being "education is important." Parents demonstrated the value of education by establishing routines and habits, taking grades seriously, working with the classroom teacher on in-class behavioral issues, taking time to help with homework to the best of their ability, and exhibiting pride in their children for their college-student identities.

The value of education was also demonstrated by restrictions that parents placed on their children. For example, despite a desire to have a job, parents prohibited their children from being employed. The message was, "You need to focus on your education, then you'll get a better job later," and "If you get a job, you won't want to focus on school—you'll just want to work more hours to make more money." Parents felt that it was their role as parents to provide what a child needed and sometimes wanted. They felt that it was one of the roles as their children to focus on school and removed a potential obstacle to education by ensuring that children had all they needed. Good grades secured that they could on occasion, get what they wanted.

Verbal messages about the importance of education were relayed by parents, and their children were able to retain these messages as evidenced by their ability to recall these messages and repeat them to me.

One participant remembers her mother saying:

> My mother…honestly this kind of sums everything up. My mother always said that "We are not rich, and the only inheritance we can leave you is a good education." It's mainly been drilled. Neither of them actually finished college. They had some experience but in Mexico. It was always, "Get a good education, and you can find a good job. Be successful. It will give you a lot of opportunities. Just really focus on your education." That was really the top priority.

Parents, as cited in the literature, used their personal stories as cautionary tales and life lessons as reasons for why their children should stay in school. A number of the participants of the focus group reported hearing parents saying, "You need to get an education because you don't want to have to be working like me." One parent shared her regret of not having been able to obtain a formal education and told her daughter:

> My mom would say, "Oh, you're lucky to be where you are because when I was your age my parents didn't want me to go to college." So what my mom did was at my age she ran away and had kids but like at the same time she came here and the only thing that she could do was go to a community college. So basically she's like, "Live my dream, but in your own way."

Education was seen as a way up and a way out of the family's current economic reality. Students were aware that after completing their education, they would be expected to care for their parents later in life. Participants were acutely aware of the fact that dropping out was not an option for them. Students did not want to join the ranks of family members who had started college but not earned their degree. A female student was told, "Don't drop out. Don't be like your sister [who dropped out]. You have to finish." Again, there was the issue of positive rivalry and comparison to successful cousins with messages like, "Be like your cousin, Moses. He went to college."

Participants also expressed an interest in "finishing" college to fulfill their parents' dreams, to save face for the family, to express gratitude for how their parents raised them, and because they didn't want to waste familial financial resources. One participant said, "I would feel bad if I dropped out and they spent all that money. Like some people don't care and they just figure, 'Oh well,' because their parents have money. Try saying that in a Latino household!"

UMASS students received more than messages about the importance of education from their families. Additionally, they were fortified with cultural capital as well.

Manifestations of Cultural Capital

Aspirational Capital. Participants continued to express a desire to complete their degree programs during the data collection process. One participant said that she had to finish school. She said she had aspirations of "Earning my B.A., going to grad school and making money. I ultimately want to give my mom things and give my mom money. That's important for my mom, too." Later on in the in-depth interview, that same participant stated, "The only option I ever had was to go to college. College was the ticket—it was going to be the defining thing. I want to go beyond everything she [her mother] wanted to be."

A student who had aspirations of pursuing a nursing degree shared her aspirations to be a provider for her parents, saying

> It's not just the expectations that my parents have for me. I want to get out of here, and I want to be a nurse. I want to give my parents more than they have ever given me, and I just want to have them sit, relax, take it easy.

At UMASS, participant aspirations were closely tied to enhancing family life experiences, and options. Latinx students at Smith College and UMASS both seem to possess a desire and an aspiration to fulfill the dreams of their parents. The students at UMASS speak more of aspiring to obtain jobs and make money that would create comfortable lives for their parents and would create opportunities for which children could "take care" of their parents as a sort of repayment for all they feel their parents have afforded them.

One participant who wants to become a firefighter despite his mother's objections laid out a plan to inform her of his aspirations. Because his mother disapproves of his aspirations because of the risks involved and because he always follows his mother's advice, she is in a sense, an obstacle to his realizing his goals. To convince her to give her blessing for him to become a volunteer firefighter, he told her that being a firefighter and having experience caring for others in distress would enhance his chances of getting into medical school, something that she was very excited about. When he explained how the experience of being a firefighter would be related to aspects of the medical field, he not only convinced her to give her blessing, but he impressed her with his vast knowledge of firefighting and emergency rescue procedures.

Familial Capital. Without family members in close proximity, participants in this study felt the need to replicate a family structure they were familiar with. This was accomplished by "adopting" surrogate family members to "create" families that consisted of friends and members of support networks. At Smith College, creating such a familial structure was easier than at the university because they had one established Latina organization. The university had several Latinx organizations to choose from and participants described having to look outside of the college-sponsored multicultural organizations for support. Unlike the replication of family that took place within *Nosotras*, the ways in which the six forms of cultural capital are transmitted were not fully actualized through the surrogate families at UMASS.

A male student spoke of how a white friend of his had become for him, a father figure. He noted that he and his friend, Brian,[3] relied on one another for support and that he considered Brian somewhat to be an honorary Colombian and a member of the family. This student stated that he did not feel a need to seek out members of Latinx cultural organizations to make friends. I credit this participant's ability to create an extended family out of familial capital. This participant is no stranger to the process of inviting and welcoming extended family members and regarding family friends as members of the family. This is what he has demonstrated through his friendship with Brian.

While this participant adopted Brian into his family, another participant would adopt an entire family, her sorority sisters, into her family. This group would make up a group of women who she would refer to as her "sisters," once again exhibiting a replication of Latinx family culture. When speaking of the group she says that they check in with each other every day, and she relies on these people that are like family. "These friends have become my family. They are my home away from home."

Initially, when she told her family that she was joining a sorority, they feared that she had joined a cult while away at school. This evidenced a lack of social capital on the part of family members who did not have prior access to information regarding college groups and activities. Once she explained that the group was actually a Latina organization, her family was open to the idea of her membership and mentioned that "every one of the sisters has even met my mom!" which signifies that the members of the group were significant enough to her to introduce them to an important member of her biological family.

Linguistic Capital. During focus groups, participants told stories about their families in very animated ways. They used their entire bodies to tell the stories of individual family member idiosyncrasies. They memorized dialogue that had taken place, used dramatic pauses, imitated people within the story, and utilized facial expressions and comedic timing. Participating in the act of sharing an anecdote, these participants were embodying linguistic capital.

This phenomenon was noted during semi-structured individual interviews as well. Participants changed their voices to "play different roles" in the story they were telling and were able to retell stories that had taken place in some cases, as long as 30 years before their birth. Instead of telling a story that had happened to someone else, participants were so convincing in the story-telling, it was as if they were there as the story unfolded. These historical re-enactments were artfully done and always in the spirit of fun. I noticed that the telling of one story sparked the telling of multiple stories, especially in the focus group setting.

Navigational Capital. One male student described how his mother instills resilience and fortification to endure hostile settings. He disclosed that his mother teases him during phone calls in a good-natured way. She uses humor to provide levity when he is describing being stressed, and this type of play reminds him not to take himself so seriously. He has stated that this exchange of communication has helped him to "laugh at myself a little."

Another male student spoke of how he used adaptability as a resilience tool. Adaptability is something he learned from his father who recounted endless stories of how he had to adapt to American culture after moving here from the Dominican Republic. As a result of seeing this behavior modeled, the participant was also able to adapt to a "foreign" culture, that of UMASS, when he first arrived as a first-year student. Being able to adapt is something he credits for making his first year much easier.

A female participant drew the connection between resilience and the choice to be resilient when she said:

> There is will and what you learn. You can be taught to go to school, but that has nothing to do with wanting to do something. At the end of the day, it's up to you if you want to do something or not, if you want to finish school or not. Some people fail when they don't have the will.

Having "will" was a theme that arose during the discussion on resistance capital and utilizing voice to work against oppression.

Resistance Capital. Participants at UMASS voiced feeling the need to challenge inequality both during their time at the university and after graduation. One student talked about using resistance capital in her classes. She said, "I feel like it's my job not to be invisible in the classroom. I never noticed that before coming here. I feel like I have to work twice as hard to be here."

Another participant discussed using resistance capital when she talked about what she is considering doing after she graduates from UMASS:

> I feel I have to do some kind of work in the Springfield public schools. In the Access[4] class, the community service that we do is in Springfield, so I started to get really attached to the school system there. I just feel like I need to do something about it. I feel like I had an advantage with my mom always being there, but I see that most of the boys only have one single mother, and I see how that affects their education. I really want to do something there.

This participant spoke of challenging campus-wide inequity and taking on the UMASS administration for the restructuring of campus diversity programs:

> I did research on the VP to see what programs he cut at his former institution and I have been learning about him. And we had a meeting with him, and he was sitting at one end of the table, and I was sitting at the other. And he said, "I sense a lot of hostility in the room," as we were questioning him, and I said, "That's interesting. So do I."

This exchange was enough for the VP to seek her out after the meeting in private, assuming that she was the spokesperson for the group. She informed him that she was just someone who was concerned over what was happening with diversity on campus.

Social Capital. With a restructured diversity program on campus, participants reported feeling at a loss for being able to locate and/or utilize resources on campus. Instead of turning to the administration for this support, students turned to each other to relay campus news and social activities information. I was told that there is no better publicity for students of color on campus through word of mouth, and through that pipeline of information you can basically learn anything you want to know. One student said that resources on campus weren't easy to find, but she felt, "like I started hearing things from other people because by myself I really didn't know. It was through other students." Further, she felt as if locating resources was a mystery for Latinx students on campus:

> It was a mystery because you kind of have to find it. I keep hearing there are so many resources, but it's not until now that I know about the resources. And that's kind of my job is finding the resources, providing underrepresented students with those resources that I know about.

She remedied this issue of not having connections to resources by reaching out to fellow students by enrolling in a diversity course, decided that "instead of just sitting here in my room watching TV let me go outside and talk to somebody," "finding other minorities and hanging out" and getting involved with diversity organizations that served students of color.

Other participants talked to Latinx staff and developed relationships with as a resource for different opportunities on campus. In general, participants developed connections with those who could inform them of resources available on campus since these weren't conscientiously advertised to students of color.

Students at the university were able to describe parental engagement as a foundation that parents built during early childhood and extended through college through moral support. The cultural messages that they learned were regarding the importance of education for increasing advancement opportunities. Another included lessons related to the lamentations of their parents regarding not having fulfilled their personal dreams of obtaining a formal education. Participants employed these messages by developing aspirations that would strive to support their parents as repayment for their sacrifices and to fulfill their parents' dreams of higher education. Finally, through data derived from the focus group and in-depth interviews, participants revealed that students at UMASS were utilizing all six forms of cultural capital.

Notes

1. According to the UMASS Amherst 2017–2018 Common Data Set.
2. Slang for paraphernalia.
3. Pseudonym.
4. Pseudonym for the group she is involved with on campus.

· 7 ·

MANIFESTATIONS OF CULTURAL CAPITAL

Participants at Holyoke Community College

Holyoke Community College (HCC) in Holyoke, Massachusetts, was founded in 1946 and is the "youngest" of educational institutions featured in this
research study. It began as a Junior College that was sponsored by the City of
Holyoke. The small college was said to have lacked the resources at the time
that were available at more traditional colleges. It started with only two staff
members: the college's founder and his secretary who shared a small room
within the space they borrowed from the local high school. Lacking the simple resources needed for the faculty who taught in the evening, the two staff
members would steal whatever erasers, pencils, and pieces of chalk that they
could.

In January 1968 the college's newly renovated campus suffered a fire and
the campus was completely lost. Despite this tragedy, the college community
worked together to ensure that work could begin again in a few days within
transitory quarters. The community worked together to bombard the Gover-
nor with correspondence that would demand that the school be rebuilt in the
town of its origin.

The college has come a long way since its founding over 70 years ago. It
now boasts a multi-million-dollar, 165-acre campus and updated technology.
The college serves over 9,000 students and is proudest of its history of origi-

nality, service to students, and a vision for continued success. Unlike students at Smith College and UMASS who would be able to live on campus, HCC does not have residential facilities, and, therefore, its students are commuters from the immediate area. Most of the participants still live at home with their parents, a distinct difference between students at Smith and UMASS, and a factor I believe to have had an impact on the data. A demographic summary[1] can be found below (Table 7.1).

Table 7.1: Holyoke Community College, Student Profile, Fall 2018.

Racial/Cultural Categories	Degree-Seeking Undergraduates (includes first-time first-year)
Nonresident aliens	107
Hispanic	2,794
Black or African American, non-Hispanic	537
White, non-Hispanic	6,234
American Indian or Alaska Native, non-Hispanic	2
Asian, non-Hispanic	322
Native Hawaiian or other Pacific Islander, non-Hispanic	2
Two or more races, non-Hispanic	429
Race and/or ethnicity unknown	322
Total	10,749

Source: Author.

Data Collection

Myriam Quiñones, the Coordinator for Multicultural Academic Services was contacted for assistance in recruiting participants for the study. Similar to what was done at the other research sites, a "Call for Participants Letter" was emailed, respondents were asked to complete the "Demographic Question-naire," and those who were deemed eligible to continue in the process were forwarded an "Informed Consent Form." A meeting was scheduled where participants were given a copy of the consent form asked questions about the nature of the study, who they could contact about the study and their rights as a participant. Participants were notified about the Likert-scale survey, and they were invited to take part in the focus group discussion.

The main contact and my liaison to the students I was working with was the aforementioned program Coordinator who has access to and rapport with a large population of Latinx students on campus. She forwarded my "Call for Participants" through email and spread news of the study through word of mouth. I believe that the latter technique utilized was the most effective at all three sites. The Coordinator identifies as Latina, Puerto Rican to be exact, and has earned a great deal of credibility and trust among the Latinx students. The Coordinator also identifies as a lesbian and her wife also worked at the institution and is an academic advisor within the Multicultural Academic Services department. They were both actively involved in taking the students they serve on educational and recreational field trips and had become surrogate parents to some of the students they serve. I was invited to hold a focus group during the meeting time of the campus's only Latinx organization on campus where I recruited participants. Similar to what had been done at Smith and UMASS, food was provided not by me but through the Coordinator's office.

A total of eight Latinx students attended the focus group. One student who was recruited outside of the focus group was invited to take part in the study but chose not to even after repeated attempts to contact her. Eight participants followed through with the process and completed data sets. The total number of participants between the focus group and in-depth interviews was eight. The focus group themes that emerged were consistent with the themes of the in-depth interviews.

Description of Parental Engagement

Since some of the participants in this study live with extended family members, the descriptions offered by CC students do not always refer to biological parents but by family who have become parental figures.

The first participant interviewed shared that her parents were together until she was five years old after which time she was raised by her mother and extended family who she respected as parents because "respect was ingrained" in her, as she stated. She described her mother as "very involved" in her education. Where grades were concerned, she was told to "do your best and try your hardest." Her mother frowned upon grades that were a "C" or lower, and there were consequences for poor grades. Her mother would take away TV watching privileges, and the time that she would normally spend playing with cousins would be reduced. There were also rewards for good grades and her mother would reward this by taking her out to eat or purchasing a small gift for her.

While her mother's work schedule prevented her from attending PTA meetings and parent teacher conferences, she was able to attend the school's open house event. A lack of attendance at these events did not diminish her involvement. She taught her daughter to be respectful to the teacher at all times because the teacher was "giving her something and helping her out." Her mother taught her never to be disrespectful to her teachers. Currently in the college setting, her mother demonstrates support and involvement through messages and encouragement. When asked about how her mother demonstrates support, the participant said:

> [When I am experiencing stress, my mother] tells me to relax, not to worry so much, that I am a smart girl, and I could do whatever. She really just helps me to relax because I am a very anxious person. So when she sees that I'm getting that way, she will sit me down and talk to me, tells me that I am doing a good job and not to worry.

Like other parents described in the research study, this participant's mother boasts about her daughter, is looking forward to her graduation, and has voiced the sentiment that she is proud of her.

Another participant that was interviewed shared that both of her parents were college-educated and deeply involved in her education. There was no rhyme or reason to who helped her with homework. Both parents assisted with homework and the parent who helped would be the parent who returned home from work first. There were no consequences for bad grades. If she didn't do well in school, her parents would say, "Just do better next time." There were also no rewards for good grades. She shared:

> [My parents demonstrated involvement in my early education by] attending open houses. Involvement was more at home. They would go through my back pack, and up until middle school, they could just walk up and talk to my teachers since they worked in the same school.

This participant shared that she felt her parents didn't attend PTA meetings because it was a "White parent thing." As a college student, she felt that her parents are proud of her, and she was invested in making them proud.

One participant shared that her mother demonstrated involvement because she didn't pressure her to stay in school when she wanted to drop out. Rather, her mother talks to her in such a way the participant shared that "it helps me to refocus and go for what I want."

A different participant shared that her parents motivated her by present-ing a bleak outlook of what her life would look like if she didn't complete her education. "Do you want to work at Home Depot all your life?" they would ask her.

I would be remiss if I didn't introduce the data that reported Latinx par-ents who were uninvolved and disengaged in the education of their children. Some participants in the study cited that they didn't have any support from their parents or that their parents felt that going to school was a waste of time when they could be employed with full-time jobs and helping to financially support the family. One participant shared that the way in which her mother was "involved" in her education was that her mother's lifestyle was evidence that education was important and that she didn't want to follow in her moth-er's footsteps. During the interview, she whispered that her mother had *vicios* (vices), and she didn't want to go down a similar path.

Employing Cultural Messages Regarding Education

For the majority of participants interviewed, the main cultural message re-garding education was that education was important and valued within the family. One parent told her daughter that "your [educational] degree deter-mines who you are." A male student was reminded that as far as family college graduates were concerned "nobody finished. I wanted to go further than they did." Another participant was told "if you want to be successful, you have to be successful in school." This was accentuated by the fact that the people im-parting this message to her were seamstresses, and she would note that their work was never-ending. They would work in the factory and then bring work home. What was demonstrated to her was that an education could provide different life options than what was available to her family. What she was told was "you have to study because you have to get out."

Messages that these students received about education were mainly that an education was vital in improving one's life situation and in providing more options. While some participants expressed wanting to make parents proud, the general sentiment was that education provides access and escape.

Manifestations of Cultural Capital

Aspirational Capital. Students at HCC brightened when they talked about the aspirations they have for their futures. After asking one participant about her aspirations, she quickly answered:

I always knew I was going to college. That was always my dream in school. Now that I am in college, I want to be a forensic psychologist. And I have another dream which is to someday buy a house and take in veterans and homeless people.

Another participant shared that she wanted to be a high school English teacher so she could use multi-media to attract students to want to read and to accommodate students with learning disabilities. She said that she wants to show kids that "reading doesn't have to be boring."

"Wanting to make my parents proud" was an aspiration for another participant who said that this was an aspiration because: "I am blessed to have the parents that I have. I credit them for who I am." Similarly, another participant said: [She] "always knew I would go to college. I can do it. I can go to college, be successful, better myself and make my mother proud."

Another participant's aspirations were very simple. After college, he simply wanted to "have a career and be a good person." A participant whose dream is to be a neonatal nurse shared that the highest degree she wanted to obtain was a master's degree. She was exuberant when she talked about premature babies. She offered statistics on the survival rates of "preemies" and likened their struggle to her struggle obtaining an education. She said that she had the same message for preemies as she does for herself which is, "You can do it! Fight! Fight hard!"

While some participants held aspirations to make their parents proud and to show gratitude for the parents that they have, other participants had aspirations to better their own lives. As evidenced in the aspirations of students, there are some whose aspirations include helping and improving the lives of strangers and the marginalized, such as veterans, the homeless, young people, and premature babies.

Familial Capital. Familial capital was an interesting phenomenon to analyze with this group in particular because most of the participants in the study still live with their families. A need to adopt new family or extended family members largely does not exist, nor is there a need to seek out people who identify as Latinx at Holyoke Community College.

While it was evident that support systems existed in the places that participants called "home," I was still curious to know where they found support at HCC and if familial capital was at play. Living at home did not necessitate a need to replicate family structure; however, participants unanimously spoke of the multicultural academic services Coordinator as if she were a surrogate mother and also included the Coordinator's wife as a source of support. This was information that was not solicited but, rather, volunteered from the participants themselves. It was notably interesting that the Coordinator's wife was mentioned without my prompting as a point of discussion. The Coordinator was especially vital for those participants without close ties to a mother figure.

When asked who they found to be a support on campus, students referenced Myriam, and I noted that she possesses the characteristics described of highly involved Latina mothers (as she herself is a mother to two daughters). When I asked one participant why Myriam was considered to be a support, she said, "She knows what classes I have taken, and she can answer my questions resourcefully. She's easy to talk to, and she checks up and checks in. She has high expectations for me, and she wants me to succeed."

Another participant stated, "Myriam is my home. A lot of students feel that way." A participant who is estranged from her mother said, "Myriam gets excited that I could be on the Dean's List. She's the reason I am staying in college. She's very demanding."

Of the Latinx cultural organization that Myriam currently advises, participants describe this group as a "little family." As one participant said:

> Educationally, we're there for each other. Emotionally, we're there for each other. There is also a sibling sort of rivalry. You want to do better, compete with each other, pick each other up. If one does good in math, we're all inspired to do good. The group is like a giant family. Yeah, we have our arguments, but they don't last long. We'll argue and then someone will kick you like to say, "I'm sorry," and then you move on.

Where participants at Smith and UMASS might not have had a family member who had gone to college, could help them navigate college, and who could communicate the expectations and milestones within college to families unfamiliar with college practices, all of the participants had this resource in Myriam—someone they considered to be a second home.

Linguistic Capital. Linguistic capital was not something reported in the focus group or in-depth interviews, but it was a part of my observations as I sat in the multicultural academic services space to wait for and interview students. The space is rarely empty, and it is rarely quiet. There always seems to be at least one student in the reception area and students speaking to Myriam in her office. In between class periods and during lunch, the office was abuzz with activity and laughter that could be heard echoing down the hallways.

Linguistic capital in the form of storytelling was a common occurrence in the office. Students would be telling stories to Myriam about something that had happened in class or something that a cultural organization member did, and the hallmarks of linguistic capital were evident. Using body language to tell the story, inflection of voice, dramatic pauses, facial effects, memorization, and use of rhythm and rhyme were all evident. If two students had been together at an event, and one was retelling a story from the event in such a way that didn't capture the moment, the other student would take over the story. A back-and-forth storytelling would take place with two storytellers allowing space for the other to enter and exit the story. It was entertaining, beautiful, fluid, and seamless to watch.

It seemed in this setting, the purpose of the storytelling was not to impart educational or moral lessons but to make others laugh and create moments of levity within the day.

Navigational Capital. One participant talked about possessing and practicing inner resilience in how she problem-solved. She would tell herself, "You're grown. You can do this," and she would set out to solve problems on her own. It was only in circumstances that she tried to solve problems on her own and was unsuccessful that she would seek out the help of others.

For another participant, living with her mother has reinforced the navigational capital she originally learned. The participant is confident that she possesses the strengths necessary to accomplish what she sets out to and said, "Now my education is for myself, and what I want to do. I am committed to my schoolwork, and I hold myself to high expectations."

A student who is not living with her mother and whose mother did not reinforce the value of education shared her story:

> I wanted to drop out after high school. My mom didn't motivate me. She never had anything to say about school and if I did good, she wasn't excited. I figured, "What's the point?" I live with my grandmother, and she thought that high school was the end. She gets happy about good grades but not excited. She feels like school is wasting your time. Sometimes I feel down and I say, "Grandma, I need to do this." She supports my decision, but she's not happy. I am in school thanks to Myriam. She gets excited when I get good grades. She gets more excited than I do. Now I feel like education is more important than you think. I value it more now, and I am proud of getting good grades.

This student's story is evidence that navigational capital can be transmitted and learned later in life with the appropriate support. It is also evidence that it can be transmitted through someone who understands Latinx culture and someone who is regarded and trusted as a family member.

Resistance Capital. Resistance capital was evidenced through the topics that participants chose to lend their voices to. After attending two cultural organization meetings, I learned that the group was currently comprised of women who took the initiative to do community service work as a group activity and really enjoyed it. It seemed important to the group that injustices against women need to be addressed and that women need to be celebrated. One woman who participated in the research study described that the men in her family want to dominate the women. She shared that she has two uncles who own businesses and tried to pressure her to drop out of school and come work for them when she was younger. It was the women in her family, she added, who advocated for her to stay in school and complete her studies.

The intersection of gender and Latinx culture are salient for these women. While many of the women have said that they are nervous about taking part in public artistic performances, several women have signed up to take part in the Spanish production of the "Vagina Monologues." HCC sponsored the monologues where one participant, Myriam, and Myriam's wife were also in the production. The proceeds from the Holyoke Community College sponsored production went to a local women's shelter. The Spanish version of the monologues would be performed in the community outside of the college. Myriam was working with the actresses to teach them the craft of acting and to get them comfortable with the material they are working with. Proceeds from this production will be going to a women's shelter as well. While they may not describe it this way, participants are engaged in the practice of working toward social change.

Social Capital. Students at HCC expressed an ease, comfort, and skill in locating the necessary resources to ensure their academic success on campus. Myriam is a large contributor to their access to resources; however, they are also cognizant of and savvy to the other resources at their disposal. Some participants are aware of how to locate and utilize these resources even before they are enrolled at Holyoke Community College. This is due in some part to pre-college programs that highlight colleges in the surrounding area. A student who participates in a pre-college program would be able to locate the actual office on campus they are looking for before a matriculated student can.

Observing the students in the campus space that is most familiar to them, I watched them act as resources for one another. This was most obvious when I observed an organizational meeting. During this meeting, the group was trying to create a list of activities that they wanted to do in the spring. When the question of how they would secure resources for an activity was raised, almost instantly, a group member would mention a personal connection they had who would be able to provide the necessary resources at little to no cost. From sitting with the group for no more than one hour, I was updated on everything from the bus schedule to where I could go if I wanted to go horseback riding. It wouldn't take very long until I myself was assessed for my resource potential and asked, "Do you have any connection to the Fine Arts Center?"

The innovation that the college was founded and maintained on is clearly reflected in these students.

Note

1. According to the College's Fall 2018 Student Profile.

· 8 ·

LATINX PARENTAL ENGAGEMENT

A Portrait in Two Puerto Rican Communities

In the 2017 academic year, I worked with Mari Santiago and Daisy Rivera, two exceptional Puerto Rican students in Mount Holyoke College's (MHC) Frances Perkins (FP) Scholars Program. The FP program, similar to the Ada Comstock Scholar program at Smith College and the Davis Scholars program at Wellesley College, supports "non-traditional" age students to earn their bachelor's degrees. Mari and Daisy were exemplary students who were interested in my study, and they also were savvy networkers who had connections in the Holyoke, Massachusetts public school system.

Research Site One: Holyoke, Massachusetts

The City of Holyoke has the highest per capita population of Puerto Ricans anywhere in the country outside of the island. In 2017, the U.S. Census reported that Holyoke's population was 40,341. Of that number, 51.2% identified as Hispanic or Latino, and 43.0% identified as white. Persons with a high school diploma ages 25 years and older was reported at 79.0% and persons with a bachelor's degree or higher ages 25 and older measured at 24.1%. The median household income in dollars was $37,954, and 28.6% of Holyoke residents were reported to be living in poverty (https://www.census.gov/

quickfacts/holyokecitymassachusetts). My previous work as a Director of Middle and High School Programs at Girls Inc. of Holyoke required me to maintain close professional relationships with agency partners. Of those partnerships, schools were prominent, and I made frequent visits to Holyoke Public Schools. Once again, deficit theories regarding Latinx parental engagement were challenged as in every school, there seemed to always be a parental presence. This prompted my interest in learning more about either what these schools were doing "right," or why Latinx parents were showing up in force. My initial research questions were regarding Latinx parental resilience. I know that Latinx students face hostile environments, and that they credit their parents and caregivers for their academic success. If Latinxs face discrimination and Latinx parents are a support for Latinx students, what does Latinx parental resilience look like, and how are Latinx parents buoyed in racist systems? With that, I turned my attention to the City of Holyoke. The City of Springfield shares demographics similar to the City of Holyoke, but I am Puerto Rican, and I, too, use my social capital. Between Mari, Daisy, and myself, we had more connections in Holyoke than we did in Springfield. Additionally, Holyoke had made headlines for the fact that their schools were under receivership. These factors made Holyoke the ideal place for our research.

Mari and Daisy divided their work by interviewing parents of elementary and middle school students and parents of high school students. They conducted 21 phenomenological interviews, and one focus group. To compensate parents for their time, and in the interest of not replicating the oppressive manifestation of exploitation, each participant received $10 in cash thanks to the generosity of the Harap Family, who funds small research projects at MHC. The interviews were conducted on site at the school or at the public library. The focus group was conducted at MHC with a dinner for participants, and Mari had arranged for transportation, knowing that lack of access to transportation is a deterrent for families in attending events.

The findings from the interviews and focus group mirrored my own research findings in relation to Latinx parental engagement with parents saying that they check their children's book bags and prioritize homework when their children come home from school. Two themes were evident in regard to completion of homework. First, parents helped with homework to the extent that they could, and if students reported not being assigned any homework, they would verify that with the teacher. When asked about their rationale for creating specific routines around homework completion, focus group participants listed "organization, time management, focus, assistance with learning how to plan, and giving schoolwork" importance. Second, parents always fed children and/or allowed for time to "decompress" before they were expected to do homework. This practice of balancing self-care for parents in elementary, middle, and high school levels were consistent with my research and what parents of college students also advocated for—take care of yourself and take care of your schoolwork. Students at the college level reported that their parents called to make sure that they were eating and taking care of themselves as this healthy behavior facilitated academic success. In my own life, my mother would call me daily to ensure that I had eaten and gotten enough rest, It was common for her to call me before I departed for my *doctoral-level* classes to remind me that "breakfast is the most important meal of the day, and you can't learn if you're hungry."

Another interesting finding was the manifestation of cultural capital. In my initial study I had built upon the cultural capital of familial capital to show that college students did utilize what they learned about familial capital from their parents and families *and* they replicated familial structures. The parents in Holyoke also expressed how they expected teachers to be an extension of biological family to a replicated family member. One participant shared that she felt "The role of the teacher is like a second mom because she is with the students every day and they are under her care. It's like having a second mother for them." Several parents shared that the teacher's role should be more of a disciplinarian. One participant shared that a teacher should "be like a parent and take care of them [students] as their own." Other participants spoke of teachers as people who would share parent qualities such as being supportive, providing guidance, and teaching basic manners. In the focus group, participants shared that teachers should wear many hats including, but not limited to "mentor, "shrink," confidante, nurse, second mom, advocate, and guide."

The parents in Holyoke had either been born on the mainland U.S. or had moved from Puerto Rico for at least five years or longer, allowing enough opportunity for them to get assimilated to, or at least familiar with, the expectations around parental engagement in the U.S. public school system. I was curious to find out if a value for education is something that is *learned*, or if it is an inherent trait in Latinxs, and in this case, Puerto Ricans. I was able to travel to San Juan, Puerto Rico to begin investigating this question.

Research Site Two: Playita, San Juan, Puerto Rico

In the summer of 2018, a partnership between Mount Holyoke College and the Municipality of San Juan, Puerto Rico facilitated a weeklong STEM program for girls in the barrio of Playita. Playita had made headlines after Hurricane Maria as residents hung a sign from an overpass that read "Playita necisista ayuda, comida, agua."[1] Residents said that they had waited more than a week after the hurricane for assistance, and the barrio's proximity to a lagoon made the floodwaters especially problematic. In late July of 2018, Dr. Jared Schwartzer, my colleague at Mt. Holyoke and I traveled down to San Juan to meet with the Mayor of San Juan, Carmen Yulín Cruz, to fulfill her request for a STEM program for girls in Playita. We had been calling contacts to develop the program and secure resources, but to no avail. I remembered that in my own life, "old school" Puerto Ricans do business face-to-face, not through texts or email. Additionally, San Juan and the resources in the Municipality were maxed. The Hurricane's aftermath was still very evident even from the air as we flew over the island and could still see blue tarps covering precarious rooftops. On land, it didn't take long to see the devastation. A downed billboard soon became our indication that we were approaching the barrio of Playita.

In April 2018, Mayor Cruz visited Mount Holyoke College and the City of Holyoke. It was during her trip to MHC that I was able to speak with her about the summer program, and where at which, I would earn the nickname "Wonder Woman." We were able to see the Mayor again in San Juan in July 2018, through Jossie Valentin, a mutual colleague and friend. On the day we met with Yulín, we were instructed to meet her at the opening of a new community center in the middle of Playita. The community center was solar powered and housed water filtration systems, a kitchenette, first aid kits, solar powered lights, inflatable rafts, machetes, brooms, and work gloves—essential items in the event of another hurricane. Yulín was in the middle of speaking to residents of Playita when she turned and noticed me standing in a corner. "Wonder Woman!" she said, as she walked toward me with arms outstretched for a hug. After the crowd cleared, we were able to talk about the program with some parents and leaders from the community, and what Jared and I were trying to accomplish in months was taken care of in a matter of hours. By the end of the day, we had access to a Superintendent, school principal, use of space and access to school staff, transportation, and meals, not to mention the full support of the Municipality. We had been able to tour the school that would be the site of the pilot program. A Microsoft School, the space is impressive with bright hallways and wet labs, and yet, the effects of Maria were still present. In a small courtyard near the school's entrance stands a breathtaking Flamboyan tree. Inside the school, there is a poster with pictures of staff in front of the Flamboyan tree over the course of months. Amanda Diaz, the Principal of EMCT explained that the tree had been devastated during the hurricane, and the staff decided to take the same picture every month in front of the tree. Moving her finger across the poster, she said "the tree was destroyed, but look what happened—the tree started to come back." The connection was clear—the spirit and strength of the Flamboyan was symbolic of the Puerto Rican people, her students, and her staff. Classrooms still had ceiling tiles that were missing from the hurricane. As a tropical depression was expected that weekend, all materials were covered in plastic. Only recently did the last of the students get electrical power back to their homes. Amanda explained that it was a traumatic time and she was convinced the people were also suffering from PTSD. The school has a beautiful rooftop, but the decision was made that students would not utilize it. The Escuela del Deporte next door suffered damage visible from EMCT's rooftop. The school's tin roof was sliced in half and precariously perched. One more strong storm, and the roof would be gone.

Two days later, we hosted an information session in the community center for a full house. We filled two pages with names of parents and girls who wanted to participate in the program, but I was not convinced that parents would be so willing to entrust their daughters to us so easily. When I served as Director of Middle and High School Programs at Girls Incorporated of Holyoke, we had to convince parents in the predominantly Puerto Rican city to allow their daughters to travel from Holyoke to Amherst—a distance of a little more than 20 miles away. Holyoke parents felt that since they didn't know anyone in Amherst, sending them to another city was like sending them to another planet. "Would we encounter the same issue?" I wondered. Historically, Puerto Rican families are close knit, and having just met us two days prior, Jared and I weren't exactly known entities.

On August 4, 2018, Jared and I boarded a plane to San Juan to begin the STEM program. That Sunday night, we met with the Principal of the Escuela Especializada de Matematicas Ciencias y Tecnologia (EMCT), Amanda Diaz, from the site we would be working from, and three of EMCT's teachers, Gretchen Torres, Ivangs Rivera, and Alex Tirado. Over dinner, we got to know one another and discuss not only our personal passions and interests, but our excitement for what the girls would have access to over the upcoming week. We arrived at the dinner as strangers, but left the restaurant as colleagues, and over the week, became friends.

On Monday, August 6, 2018, Jared, my sister Anna, and I met in the hotel lobby, each of us a bundle of excited energy to begin the program. Later in the day, we would be joined by Shani Mensing, a Mount Holyoke College colleague. We arrived at the school at around 7 am. Jared and Anna buzzed around the school with Gretchen, Ivangs, and Alex, unloading our car of supplies, program t-shirts, and gift bags for the girls. Parents from Playita were texting to let me know their daughters were excited and they wanted to make sure we were coming. When I left the building, clipboard in hand and backpack over my shoulders, I boarded the bus with the EMCT guidance counselor headed for Playita. My shoulders shook as the bus went over bumps and made tight turns onto thin streets. As I looked out the window, I could still see effects from Maria with boarded up windows and broken rooftops. I wondered how many girls would show up on the first day. Would they have fun? Had Jared and I done enough to create a strong program? Would we be giving the community what they needed, and not what we thought they'd want from our privileged ivory tower vantage point? When the driver pulled up the side entrance of the center, my heart dropped. No one was standing outside. When I walked up the ramp through the open white gated door, I saw girls smiling at me, some who I met in July and some who I'd never seen. They were prepared for the week of STEM camp as if they were ready for the first day of school. Two girls had a single colorful bow perfectly perched on the tops of their heads. But they were not alone—the tentative salutations of the summer information session were replaced with warm embraces "Wonder Woman!" some said, and I felt as though I was receiving a hero's welcome. They smiled and grabbed my arm as they told me how important the program was and as they thanked me for all of the work. The mothers and female community members of Playita took attendance, kissing the girls before they left the center. As I boarded the bus to head back to EMCT, I could feel a smile spreading across my face, my heart pounding even harder now, not with fear, but with purpose. As I looked out of the square school bus window, I saw the mothers of Playita waving enthusiastically and blowing goodbye kisses at our departing bus.

"Of course!" I thought. "*This* is Latinx parental engagement, too."

Jared and I were aiming for a participant pool of 20–25 students. As we communicated with Nilsa Medina, the Playita community liaison while we planned the program, she told us that she secured parental commitments from 22 girls. From the bus, Jared texted:

"How many?!"

I smiled as I texted "22!" All of the girls and their families who committed their time—but more—entrusted their daughters, granddaughters, and nieces to us, were all on the bus.

The girls were singing on the bus, some talking to each other, and I visited briefly with the one or two who were quietly occupying their own seats. When we pulled up to the school, we were met with the applause and cheers of not only the program staff, but by every teacher and staff person in the school. Before we stepped off the bus, I wanted to try a call and response with the girls. I explained that I would say "Cientificas!"[2] and they would respond "Presente!"[3] Using all my might, I bellowed, "Cientficas!" Half-heartedly, they responded. But I was determined to stay on the bus and try again until the teachers could hear them. More surprises awaited inside the building as Mayor Cruz, her staff, and local media were on hand to visit and report on the pilot program. Yulín hugged girls and visited each science experiment station to look on, smiling all the while and marveling at what the girls were experiencing. We were all invited to dinner at City Hall, a tour of Mayor Cruz's office, and to assist "7 Quillas," the local conservation group, with the release of the last of the leatherback turtles of the season to the sea. As these activities were not on the official schedule, I worried about how we would get parental consent so late in the day for students to be out well past our scheduled return time. There have been teachers who I have worked with over the years during my time in public education, who seemed to subscribe to the deficit mentality that Latinx parents generally can't be reached by phone and calls to them go unreturned. Within a matter of minutes, we had the consent of 21 parents. The last parent gave her consent but had to be reached with a personal phone call. We learned that parents in the community are on WhatsApp and are very responsive to messages through that platform. The first full day of the program ended around 10:00 pm and I wasn't sure what I would find when I returned to Platyita. Although it was late, there were parents and community members there, welcoming the girls back and asking them about their first day.

I returned to debrief with the Mt. Holyoke team, and I wondered if the first day's attendance and participation was a fluke. I expected that the next day's attendance might look different, and perhaps we would lose girls throughout the week. Jared and I would have considered the program a success if we ended on Friday with 15 girls. The routine on day two was similar to the first day; grab my clipboard and water bottle and board the bus, once again holding my breath as we approached the Center. On Tuesday, the girls were outside and buzzing. They were wearing the t-shirts that Jared and I had designed, and they looked happy. As I entered the building, I hugged my way through the crowd to greet the parents taking attendance. Once again, we had 22 girls. We would have 22 girls through the week, and day after day it was the same scene: grab my water and clipboard, board the bus, and have the mothers of Playita blowing kisses as we pulled away. I had to leave extra time in the morning because parents wanted to tell me about how excited their daughters were, and they wanted to hear more about the experiments they had heard about. On the second day that we boarded the bus, I gathered my breath to yell "Científicas!" and they matched my efforts, "Presente!" On the second day, I directed the girls to the garden at EMCT. As the teaching staff and I had planned, I asked "Donde esta Jared?"[4] The girls looked around at one another and were puzzled as to Jared's whereabouts. They heard "Buenos dias!"[5] and looking up in the direction of the EMCT rooftop was Jared and my sister, Anna. They giggled as they pointed at their teachers on a rooftop. "Que es esto?"[6] Jared asked as he held out an egg. "Un huevo!"[7] they yelled. Jared let go of the egg to the horror of the students who watched as the egg succumbed to the ground below. "Que pasó?"[8] he asked. We told the girls that their job on this day was to create systems to prevent their eggs from cracking when we dropped them from the roof. Inside the building, the girls hurried to their stations and designed parachutes, baskets, put eggs inside of filled balloons and wrapped balloons in cotton. The next morning, the girls waited with excited anticipation as Jared and Anna dropped each team's egg. To the delight of our group, every egg survived.

When we were back at Mt. Holyoke, I had told Jared about my idea to end the week with a science fair. This science fair would be different. I remembered that my research and existing literature cited that low parent attendance at school events were not due to disinterest but to inconvenience. We weren't going to ask the parents to come to the science fair—we were going to bring the science fair to them. We had to hold the fair on Thursday as Yulín wanted to attend and couldn't attend a science fair on Friday. The Mayor's assistants, Gloriana Salgado and Tito Otero had asked me what I needed. It was a bold ask, but I told them I needed six six-foot tables, some chairs, a tent, and a sound system. When I arrived the Center, Municipal staff were already hard at work, unfolding tables, putting up the tent and asking what else they could do to be of service. The street was closed off for the event. The Mayor was on her way. Let me say that again. The Mayor of the largest municipality on the island of Puerto Rico had dedicated staff and resources for 22 girls. 22 girls from a barrio that less than a year prior was in desperate need of food and water. Now, they were about to display the hydraulic arms made of cardboard, the LED boxes they could use in future crises, balloon powered cars, paper towers, kitchen chemistry, and egg drop kits. Tito and I, along with other staff members unloaded my car of delicate science fair projects and carefully set them on tables as the EMCT bus pulled up. Girls went directly to their stations to review the notes they had prepared for their presentations. Men from the neighborhood circled the projects and asked, their eyes filled with amazement asking "Las chicas hicieron esto?"[9] I replied that at the program, we referred to them as *scientists*, and yes, they did. Yulín arrived shortly after the school bus and visited with each team to hear about their projects. When she reached the cardboard hydraulic arm station, the wide-eyed look she gave to Jared let us know that we had done our job. Yulín had asked how we got so many parents and families to attend the fair when attendance at other events had been low. That was easy to answer—we just had to bring the science fair to them. The science fair concluded with an awards ceremony. Yulín handed each girl a backpack filled with school supplies along with a certificate of completion signed by Mount Holyoke College President Sonya Stephens. Before the crowd dispersed, I had one more thing to do.

Standing under the shelter of the tent, as rain clouds waited menacingly above me, I drew in a long breath. "Cientificas!" I called. "PRESENTE!" they bellowed back. Their reply echoed through the tiny barrio, going up and down side streets, and entering open spaces. We started the program with 22 girls unsure of their place in the sciences and ended with 22 confident scientists.

Everything I knew and had researched about Latinx parents came alive in San Juan. Were they invested in education? Yes. Parents had signed statements of commitment stating that they would ensure their child's attendance for the week. Mothers took attendance every single morning of the program, blew kisses at our bus, and met us at the end of the day—no matter how late it was. Parents thanked us every chance they got for the opportunity the program provided for their girls. Were they involved in the education of their children? Yes. The involvement wasn't "traditional," as it relates to how Latinxs are expected to assimilate on the mainland. Children were rested, fed, arrived at the program with everything we asked them to bring (their Mount Holyoke bags, program t-shirt and Municipal ID badges), and they were ready to get to work as soon as the bus arrived at EMCT. The days were very long as they almost always ended with an excursion, and the girls took full advantage of the program's offerings. It was clear that we'd be able to reach someone back home if we needed help with a girl, whether it was from family, extended family, or a community member. We had been working with parents from San Juan whose children were directly involved in the program, and people involved in the program who had their own children, some grown, some outside of the Municipality—everyone wanted to help. As the saying goes, "it takes a village," and as cliché as that may sound, in the case of Playita, it was absolutely true. We had asked for the support of teaching staff, and instead of one teacher, we got the support of three classroom teachers and the Principal, counseling staff, nursing staff, kitchen staff and literally anyone else in the building who could lend a hand. The Puerto Rican parental commitment to education is alive and well in Playita. However, a new question emerged for me as a researcher. Although I could see how parental engagement was present in Playita, I didn't have dedicated time to ask them directly about their thoughts on education.

Remembering the research Mari ad Daisy assisted with, I recalled that parents in Playita weren't subjected to the institutional racism of the U.S. public school system. To deepen my research, I "returned" to Playita this fall, in two ways. First, the partnership between EMCT and Mount Holyoke College continued as girls from the program would conduct experiments at EMCT twice a month, and they would Skype in with us. Secondly, Mount Holyoke College student lab assistants, Emely Minino Soto and Nicole Lara Granados, phoned the parents of students from the summer pilot program about their thoughts and feelings on education, and on the summer program that their daughters participated in. Several themes emerged from parental conversations regarding the program. First, parents felt that the program would help their daughters prepare for college and that they already noted their daughters were now more interested in science and were "doing better" at school, and another shared that her daughter was discouraged at school, but she felt the summer program motivated her as a student. One parent reported that her daughter had presented the experiment she conducted in the program to her science class, and another shared that the summer program experience was helping her daughters in their science classes. As for my curiosity regarding any ambivalence in sending students to the program, my suspicions were not unfounded. Nilsa Medina, community liaison for Playita, and the person who acquired parental commitments did share that some parents didn't send their children to the program because Jared and I were unknown. Once again, knowing how my family would have felt about my attendance at a program run by strangers, and remembering the reaction and resistance from parents in Holyoke, their apprehension was not a surprise to me, and it was not something that was offensive. In the interviews conducted by Emely and Nicole, safety was listed as an initial concern. One mother said that she appreciated the program because "the girls were safe," and another said

> I didn't want to do it at first because I did not know the people running the program, and I didn't trust them. They were strangers, but my mother verified the program then I took a chance on the program and it turned out good.

Data suggests that parents from marginalized identity groups who may not have had a formal education might defer making a decision (Lareau & Horvat, 1999). That would be a reasonable rationale for parental decisions not to consent to student participation in the program. However, the people of Puerto Rico were in a unique position. They were still recovering from a historically devastating hurricane and had endured promises of assistance with no follow up. Therefore, trust was certainly, and understandable an issue we faced.

Regarding their feelings, beliefs, and attitudes toward education, what was discovered did not surprise me. Parents were asked ten questions related to their level of education, occupation, reflections on their own educational experiences, familial messages about education that were imparted to them, expectations for their children around education, messages they impart about education, role of the teacher, how they support the teacher at home, the purpose of education, and feelings regarding stereotypes of Latinxs in education. Interviews ranged from 45–60 minutes and it was difficult to secure interviews for two reasons. First, scheduling was an issue with some parents at home and some at work. Two, the students placing the calls were unknown to the parents. Due to the distance and our inability to conduct the interviews in person, the lack of a developed relationship could not be mitigated.

As a Puerto Rican researcher, it was heartening to listen to the interviews and hear that the data on Latinx parental engagement supports the narratives of interviewed parents. I would like to note that similar to the study I conducted with college students on cultural capital where participants were mostly cisgender women, the parents interviewed by Emely and Nicole were entirely made up of women. The list that they were given *only* listed mothers or another female-identified relative as a main contact. Some participants had earned a bachelors and some were working in blue collar positions. The only parent who stated that school "wasn't that good" also stated that she had been educated in the United States, and not in Puerto Rico. Participants consistently shared that their own parents were strong proponents of education. Specifically answering the question of "what expectations did your family have about homework and school behavior, and what messages did your family share about education?" Research assistants recorded responses such as:

"They supported education and said to keep studying, but I did not want to continue."

"[They told me] that education was very important. I got pregnant at 21 and my parents supported me. They still told me I had to go to college and supported me throughout everything."

"They were always dependent that we did everything, and we went to college. They were attentive and never wanted us to miss school. We went every day. My parents have passed away. They would always take me to school and were always watching over my school related stuff. If I didn't study, then I wouldn't make it and they asked me "'do you want to work at McDonald's or get my education?'"

"[They taught me] to look for the best. We grew up poor and had limited resources. They told me that you have to study in order to find a good job and get what you want in life."

When asked expectations they had for their own children, and what messages they impart, their responses were related to what college students had shared in my initial study.

I don't have any problems with her [her daughter]. It is easy to communicate with her, she loves school and wants to do something she loves. She loves going to class and being with the teacher. I tell her that to get everything in life, you need an education.

"For example, when I get home, I look over their homework and stress the importance that education is important. I tell them that studying now will let them reassure their future."

"I tell them that [they have to] keep studying and keep fighting to get a good future."

"I tell them that they have to be the women of tomorrow, that they have to become better individuals."

As for their understanding of the role of the teacher in school, and what they do to support their children's classroom, teachers, participants responded:

"If the child asks questions, they have to answer. A child shouldn't go home with questions because the parents don't know the material in class. I speak in one way, but the teacher speaks in another, I support if they are giving homework, make sure they do their work. Communication with the teacher is very important."

"[The role of the teacher] is to teach and provide a good education. [My job] is teaching them and helping them with their homework."

"Teaching in a way that not all children are treated the same. Not everything is the teacher's responsibility. At home, that is where educational encouragement should start and that supports a child in school. I support the teacher by making sure my children and always studying and doing the material they are learning."

"The teacher's job is to give the students the best opportunity possible and give them material they need to know, but also make sure they understand it. They need to communicate with parents. I call and text the teachers and I send them emails. If something happens, I go straight to the school."

Participants were also asked to share their thoughts on the purpose of education:

"It's the most important thing in order to get a career. You learn to socialize with people and ask questions. Children learn independence because they don't have their mom or dad [in school]."

"To become a better person and find a job and have a more accessible life."

"To me, education helps you to move forward."

"They get better resources. They are more prepared than anyone in the world. My husband was offered employment in the U.S. and someone at the worksite said that Puerto Ricans are the best prepared."

Finally, parents were given this prompt "There are some who say that Puerto Rican Families do not care about education and do not participate in the education of their children. How would you respond to that statement?"

"They are stereotypes. I want my child to prepare for the university level and do everything to get to college."

"It's a lie. The problem is not that families aren't involved, it's the quality of schools in Puerto Rico. The schools used to be more involved with families by calling and stuff, but not anymore, I changed my daughter's school because the teacher would do nothing in the classroom."

"It is a lie because I am very attentive to my daughters' education. I want them to be professionals and push them to do good."

And this response spoke directly to the research I conducted with Latinx college students,

"In P.R., in public and private schools, we can see that parents become involved with their children's schools. Even in college, parents are always supporting their children and education and making sure that they get good grades. This is not only in P.R., but also in the whole world."

In reviewing the transcripts of the interviews, I had to remind myself that these responses were coming from parents. The similarity of the parent responses when compared to the data collected from college students in my initial study were eerily similar. It didn't take long for me to realize that I was witnessing phenomena that was generational and in addition to transcending time, these manifestations of parental engagement trespassed geography as well. Students learn the expectations of school, the rules and regulations by being immersed in that culture. As teacher candidates receive their training, those individual teachers trained with understanding the same course theories and techniques then impart that training to hundreds of children. In other words, teachers *learn* how to be teachers, and students *learn* how to be students, and the expectations all come from the same source. For example, if you gather a group of students in a classroom and ask a question, what happens? Inevitably, students begin raising their hands to get acknowledged by the teacher because that is what students have been *trained* to do. This is an example of the assimilation into the U.S. education system. The data collected in my initial study came from students who represented many different Latinx identities, and whose parents represented different Latinx countries. As I have established in chapter two, the origins of parental engagement were constructed without people of color in mind. National parent organizations established what the rules of engagement were. However, what happens to those parents who cannot, or who are not allowed to or welcomed into, those spaces? Students are trained under a national system. Parents who have the access or invitation to national parenting organizations also receive the same conformist information and training. To the best of my knowledge, there is no formal, national organization that has historically offered uniform training and information to Latinx parents on how to be engaged in the academic lives of their children.

Notes

1. "Playita needs help, food, water."
2. "Scientists!"
3. "Present!"
4. "Where's Jared?"
5. "Good morning!"
6. "What is this?"
7. "An egg!"
8. "What happened?"
9. "Did the girls do this?"

References

Lareau, A., & Horvat, E. (1999). Moments of social inclusion: Race, class, and cultural capital in family school relationships. *Sociology of Education, 71*, 39–56.

U.S. Census Bureau. (2017). Quick Facts. Holyoke, Massachusetts. Retrieved from https://www.census.gov/quickfacts/holyokecitymassachusetts

THE RECIPE FOR LATINX
STUDENT SUCCESS

The construct of parental engagement in the history of U.S. education is not a new concept. The concept can be traced back to early civilizations that recognized the importance that parents, our first educators, played in the lives of their children (Berger, 1991). The early philosophical teachings of Plato, Locke, Rosseau, Pestalozzi, and Froebel influenced the educational practices and policies that would define parental involvement for the next 90 or so years. The burgeoning interest in parent and child education of the 1920s was sustained by the U.S. government both in educational mandates and federal funding. Despite the challenges that the nation would face, support for parental engagement was unwavering. The Civil Rights Movement of the 1960s and the Civil Rights Act of 1965 would provide a golden opportunity that could have resulted in the actualization of equal rights for all people. Instead of developing school systems where students—regardless of race—would have access to equal resources, students from statistical minorities would find themselves on the precipice of an achievement gap (Love, 2004). The Elementary and Secondary Education Act was also introduced in 1965, and it would, in part, clarify and support parental engagement and would re-emerge in the 2002 No Child Left Behind Act. Despite legislation that was outwardly and seemingly progressive toward closing the achievement gap and investing in all students, Latinx students did not benefit from the spirit of these laws.

Ingredients to Success

While caring teachers are factored in Latinx student academic success (Antrop-González, Velez, & Garrett, 2005), the acts of racist teachers (Behnke, Piercy, & Diversi, 2004), and the negative perceptions that teachers and administrators have about poor Latinx parents influence interactions that are negative and patronizing (Ceballo, 2004). Teachers and administrators, who follow the construct that white, middle-class parental engagement is the standard for parental engagement, perceive that Latinx parents do not care about the educational outcomes of their children (Chrispeels & Rivero, 2001; Valdés, 1996). Parental engagement can be seen as a means of cultural capital (Grolnick & Slowiaczek, 1994; Ibanez, Kuperminc, Jurkovic, & Perilla, 2004), and may not be a form of cultural capital that Latinx parents have access to. What is valued as parental engagement is associated with the construct of parental involvement and these practices include homework help and presence at school events (Auerbach, 2006; Delgado-Gaitán & Trueba, 1991; López, 2001; Valdés, 1996). While the scholarship of Epstein (1996) attempted to advance the thinking regarding how to get parents more involved in education and offered insight into the reasons why some parents could not be as involved, the PTA's interpretation of that work called for assimilation. The PTA's six standards for school and family partnerships do not fully grasp the specific and unique realities of the Latinx parental population. While it is an honorable goal for school and parent partnerships to welcome all families, communicate effectively, support student success, speak up for every child, share power, and collaborate with community, not all families have the necessary resources to equally achieve these goals. If Latinx parents who are undocumented immigrants are in a position of powerlessness (Young, 1990), how would schools empower parents to be advocates for their children? While the PTA sets a standard for effective communication that is "two-way," it assumes that the communicators are equal parties on a level playing field when research indicates that teachers see themselves and not Latinx parents, as the "experts" on the subject of Latinx students (Yosso, 2005).

Equality in education is not achieved by a pretense that teachers consider Latinx parents as equal partners. When educators claim to be color*blind*, they admit to rendering their Latinx students as invisible. The inability to enact a color *consciousness* that appreciates and affirms the differences and assets in Latinx parental engagement is detrimental to building truly meaningful partnerships between teachers and Latinx parents. Schools acknowledge having Latinx pupils and their parents through a deficit perspective and can theorize about what's missing but fail to acknowledge what Latinx parents add and offer to their children's education. The definitions of parental engagement agree that it refers to a parent's ability to offer support and resources regarding the education of their children. Latinx parents fulfill that definition, and yet, they are not regarded as actively engaged, interested, involved, or committed to the education of their children despite the data that renders their parenting styles as effective. White parents have an impact on student learning through their parenting styles, and theirs has been the standard on parental involvement. The common denominator here is race, and as Justice Harry Blackmun stated, "in order to get beyond racism, we must first take account of race. There is no other way." (*Regents of University of CA v. Bakke*, 1978, p. 257). How are race and racism relevant to the exclusion of Latinx parents in the discourse on parental involvement?

This book is in no way, the cure all or "magic bullet" for all that ails Latinx students in education. Latinxs have been the target of racism and race-related discrimination since their arrival in the United States. As far back as the era of colonization (although Latinxs are subjected to colonization every day), Latinx people have been enslaved, exploited, marginalized and segregated by policies, practices, and borders. In the United States, Latinx people have been subjected to an endless barrage of stereotypes and on the receiving end of the ire of "Americans." We have been called "bad hombres," seen as gang members, drains on the United States government, and terrorists in a migrant caravan. These stereotypes and false perceptions scapegoat Latinx peoples while every day oppression is not held accountable.

Missing from the contemporary discourse on Latinxs is not what we *take* from the United States, but what we have to *offer*. As an educator, I can only speak to what Latinx parents, families, and communities have to bring to the canvas of the American educational system. Theorists like Sólorzano and Yosso (2001) write about the cultural capital that Latinxs bring and transfer to their children. In my own research and expanding on the research and contributions of Yosso, my early research found that Latinx college students in three different educational settings did manifest aspirational, familial, linguistic, navigational, resistance, and social capital. Latinx college students spurred each other on, gathered to tell stories to one another (oftentimes to boost morale), helped one another to traverse the bureaucracy of higher education, fought against injustice wherever and whenever they encountered it, and they were able to use their human resources to meet their goals.

My own research shows that they take familial capital and replicate familial structures, adopting roommates and friends into their families, developing family roles (matriarchs and siblings), and that they repay the debt of sacrifices their parents made for the sakes of the education with "finishing capital" to complete the journey toward education and a better life that their parents started. Participants in the doctoral study never used the word *graduation* to refer to the completion of their college careers, but instead referred to *finishing*. When I questioned their use of the term, they made it clear that their parents had made great personal sacrifices for their children's educations, and in turn, they were going to "finish" what their parents had started. The struggles and strengths are transformed into skill sets that have helped Latinx students to succeed in educational settings. I would argue that *all* marginalized racial groups bring strengths to education, and as educators, the burden is ours to discover what those are to enhance not only the educational experiences of students of color, but to enrich the academic lives of every one of our students regardless of their social identities, marginalized, or privileged statuses. Educators at every level can utilize Latinx cultural strengths to change the future of education. Given the increasing population of Latinxs in this country, and the fact that Latinxs will soon become the racial majority, the critical mass of Latinxs in our schools and the issues and strengths we bring, can no longer be brushed aside. In the concluding pages, I will share my thoughts on what each educational level can offer to support Latinx students, and hopefully, this spurs thoughts on how we can assist all students who have been traditionally marginalized.

The Recipe for Success

In chapter two of this book, I shared the origins of parental engagement and how that engagement was designed and introduced as a tool of assimilation. The initial teachings and lessons on parental engagement were not designed with people of color in mind, and therefore largely represent a white population of parents. "Standard" methods of parental engagement such as attendance at PTO meetings, presence in the school, and attendance at open house events are viewed as the dominant way for parents to demonstrate engagement. However, research on the contributions of Latinx parental engagement betray what has long since been seen as the "norm" in parental engagement. Methods of Latinx parental engagement should be included as examples for all parents in how to participate in the education of their children. If familial capital is a form of capital utilized and transmitted by Latinxs, teachers and schools should consider how to replicate those systems so that education is culturally recognizable.

In my own teaching, I found that parents were my greatest allies. If I understood a student's home life, I had a secret ingredient to what could help them to succeed. I made it a practice to regularly call and/or contact families. My first call home was *always* a call with good news. As a parent with a young child, I am not sending just a human being into the school building every day, I am sending my heart as well as all of my hopes and dreams for the future. While I certainly know that my Anna is not perfect, she is also someone I greatly admire (even at the age of six), and I want everyone inside of her school walls to understand how precious she is. Why would I not believe that parents of my students believe the same of their own children? I have shared that for some Latinx parents, they believe that the role of the teacher is to act as a second parent. With that expectation, Latinx families are inviting us into their familial capital in the consideration of us as sharing their children. I have long heard my teaching colleagues complain about not being able to reach parents as if a non-working telephone was a barbed wire fence. As educators we need to get creative about how to contact Latinx parents using cultural knowledge of what Latinxs value and need. If you can't call parents, visit their homes. If you are opposed to home visits, consider planning a gathering in a local park. Invite not only the parents of your students, but their grandparents, siblings, and extended family. We have always expected families to enter "our" territory, and for parents without advanced degrees (Lareau, 2011), this can be a very daunting and intimidating space to enter. Education is not an arena in which there should be "thems" and "uses." There are no enemies here. Therefore, we need to meet parents where they are at, as evidenced in the successful attendance of parents in the barrio of Playita in San Juan. How can we expect parents to attend an event that they cannot secure transportation to? How can we expect parents to attend an open house if they are only offered twice a year and both occurrences are in the evening? This causes some parents a heartbreaking choice of attending a school event or losing a job shift. What parent doesn't long to cheer their child on during their school assembly performance? As evidenced in what Smith College participants shared about study break packages, and knowing that Latinxs utilize aspirational capital, Latinx parents do not want their children to feel alone, or unsupported. Open houses can be held on weekends *and* evenings, and more than twice a year. Teachers can also consider having an open house in the communities where their students live and bring student artifacts with them.

Linguistic capital can be supported by elementary and middle school teachers asking Latinx students to share familial stories with the class and to showcase those stories as assets and contributions as pausing, timing, memorization, and attention to detail (linguistic capital) are strengths that benefits the linguistic growth of all children. Books and stories offered in the classroom should not just represent the traditional canon but should also highlight stories and accounts that are culturally recognizable. Latinx students *deserve* to know the contributions of their ancestors in the arts and sciences. For example, many Puerto Rican students don't know that their Taíno ancestors created the canoe, the hammock, and the barbecue. Latinx students should be able to see themselves and their lives in the narratives offered in their classrooms, and not just during "Hispanic Heritage Month."

As we know that Latinx parents utilize navigational and social capital, schools can form relationships with parents who have close ties to their communities to become ambassadors for the schools. As I mentioned in chapter four, parents of Holyoke and Playita were reluctant to allow their children to participate in summer programs because the adults running the programs were unknown to them. It was only until a family or community member could vet and verify the program coordinators that parents were willing to allow their children to particulate. While teachers certainly do not have the time to be the primary communicators on events taking place at school and do not have the time to orient all families on the resources offered at the school or district level, we can educate a small but critical number of parents to share this information with other families.

We know that Latinx students learn resistance capital, and anyone who has worked with young people know that they have a strong sense of justice. Instead of educators first viewing students as "troublemakers" when the are merely questioning practices that they deem to be unfair, we can invite young people into decision making practices where they actually have decision making power and are not serving on boards and committees in a token capacity.

Parents in both Holyoke and Playita felt that there was a great deal of school and parental contact when their children were in elementary school, but that waned one their children entered high school, almost as if high school students no longer needed the support of their parents. For parents who have not earned a high school diploma or a college degree, some of the practices and expectations of high school can be foreign to them. Educators in high school should begin talking to Latinx students about college as soon as possible. These conversations with first year high school students should not focus around the schools they may or may not be able to gain access to, but students should be supported in the dreams and goals that they have for their future. As one student in an upward bound program once told me "I know that I might not get into Harvard, but I just want to apply and try for myself." Every student has the right to do their best and be supported in actualizing their dreams.

In terms of familial capital, once again teachers should understand that parents are their greatest assets in securing the success of their students. If a parent is not present or supportive in the life of their child (as is sometimes the case with Latinx parents just as any other parents from other racial groups), the teacher can assume the role of a role model and mentor. Some Latinx students who have opted out of school have cited the discouragement of a teacher as the main reason for this. Teachers have an opportunity to assume a different role in the lives of Latinx students.

In terms of navigational capital, schools should assume more responsibility in explaining what happens in college and what the opportunities and challenges are so that they can be supported by their families without their families experiencing a segregation or educational chasm that college some-times creates between first generation Latinx college students and their families. Consistent and early information regarding the college application and FAFSA process should be discussed as well as the college entrance exams and how students can find affordable support for those. For example, schools can assist families to establish a shared vocabulary around what a major, advisor, and deans are as well as what their roles are. This alleviates the stress of students having to constantly interpret their college experiences for their parents and caregivers.

Just as students rely on teachers, educators can also tap into the rich expanse of Latinx cultural capital to help in determining best practices to reach parents and communities.

Data collected and analyzed from Smith College, UMASS Amherst, and Holyoke Community College are directly aligned with the literature available on the positive outcomes of parental engagement. Additionally, it also illuminates the issue that unfortunately higher education creates chasms between first-generation students and their families. Despite the fact that she did not have a formal education, my Mother was the smartest person I ever met. The difference between us was that an institution gave me a piece of paper to validate my intellect.

Participant narratives regarding post-elementary and secondary parental engagement suggest that first-generation families abilities to help with homework ends at the point at which they completed their own educations. First-generation Latinx students pass through an interesting portal once they (as often was the case in my study), complete their FAFSA forms all by themselves. I know first hand, that a first-generation student will always be a first-generation student. I was a first-generation college student, filling out a FAFSA by myself at the kitchen table, and completely unprepared for the SAT, and my college interview. It felt as if I was navigating my entire college application process in the dark, from how to structure my application to what to wear to my interview. Having successfully navigated the college application process, I was then called upon to help my sister and my nieces, and would learn to become a bridge to cross to the other side of where we had started. I was a first-generation masters program student, educating myself on graduate admissions requirements and standardized tests like the GRE and MAT, and how to write an essay compelling enough to grab the attention of admissions officers. I was a first-generation doctoral program student, submitting my personal statement and a body of academic work I had written, planning for the group and individual interviews, and combating imposter syndrome at every turn. I was a first-generation faculty member, trying to learn how to write and submit manuscripts, develop research programs, craft start up package budgets, and submit my first book. Instead of imagining myself on a ladder, I imagine myself on a bridge, using my education and vocation as a teacher to help others across.

Latinx parents and families must be invited to stand on that bridge with us, as equals and experts on the lives of their children. Latinxs from all parts of the country, those who were born in the U.S. or in other Latin-American countries appear to possess an inherent value for education, regardless of education status.

As we know the Latinx population is booming and that growing population is entering U.S. schools at steady rates, we need to work in concert with the various stops along the educational interstate to scaffold Latinx parental and student understandings of higher education. Colleges and Universities who will also continue to see increasing numbers of Latinx students need to reconsider the ways in which Latinx families are invited into the life of the college and have an honest accounting of policies and practices that are exclusionary. While higher education institutions typically have one "Chief Diversity Officer," colleges should consider positions that would work closely with Latinx parents and other racial minority groups to involve families in the lives of college students. Additionally, colleges need to understand and rectify the ways in which our students of color are consistently re-traumatized by the system of racism and have to navigate the system of oppression while simultaneously learning to thrive and survive on unfamiliar territory. At every turn, we need to remember that Latinx parental engagement, manifested at all levels of education, can be models for how to create communities in our own spaces and to enhance the lives of *all* of our students.

References

Antrop-Gonzalez, R., Velez, W., & Garrett, T. (2005). Donde estan los estudiantes Puertorriquenos/os exitosos? [Where are the academically successful Puerto Rican students?]: Success factors of high-achieving Puerto Rican high school students. *Journal of Latinos & Education, 4*(2), 77–94.

Auerbach, S. (2006). "If the student is good, let him fly": Moral support for college among Latino immigrant parents. *Journal of Latinos & Education, 5*(4), 275–292.

Behnke, A. O., Piercy, K. W., & Diverei, M (2004). Educational and occupational aspirations of Latino youth and their parents. *Hispanic Journal of Behavioral Sciences, 26*(1), 16–35.

Berger, E. H. (1991). Parent involvement: Yesterday and today. *The Elementary School Journal, 91*(3), 209–219.

Ceballo, R. (2004). From barrios to Yale: The role of parenting strategies in Latino families. *Hispanic Journal of Behavioral Sciences, 26*(2), 171–186.

Chrispeels, J., & Rivero, E. (2001). Engaging Latino families for student success: How parent education can reshape parents' sense of place in the education of their children. *Peabody Journal of Education, 76*(2), 119–169.

Delgado-Gaitán, C., & Trueba, H. (1991). *Crossing cultural borders: Education for immigrant families in America.* (ERIC Document Reproduction Service No. ED334318).

Epstein, J. L. (1996). Perspectives and previews in research and policy for school, family, and community partnerships. In A. Booth & J. F. Dunn (Eds.), *Family-school links* (pp. 209–246). Mahwah, NJ: Erlbaum.

Grolnick, W., & Slowiaczek, M. (1994). Parents' involvement in children's schooling: A multidimensional conceptualization and motivational model. *Child Development, 65*(1), 237–252.

Ibañez, G., Kuperminc, G., Jurkovic, G., & Perilla, J. (December 2004). Cultural attitudes and adaptations linked to achievement motivation among Latino adolescents. *Journal of Youth and Adolescence, 33*(6), 559–568.

Lareau, A. (2011). *Unequal childhoods: Class, race, and family life.* (2nd ed.). Berkeley, CA: University of California Press.

López, G. (2001). The value of hard work: Lessons on parent involvement from an (im)migrant household. *Harvard Education Review, 71*(3), 416–437.

Love, B. (2004). Brown plus 50 counter-storytelling: A critical race theory analysis of the majoritarian achievement gap story. *Equity & Excellence in Education, 37*(3), 227–246.

Regents of University of California v. Bakke. (1978). 438 US 265.

Solórzano, D. G., & Yosso, T. J. (2001). From racial stereotyping and deficit discourse toward a critical race theory in teacher education. *Multicultural Education, 9*(1), 2–8.

Valdés, G. (1996). *Con respeto: Bridging the distances between culturally diverse families and schools: An ethnographic portrait.* New York, NY: Teachers College Press.

Yosso, T. J. (2005). Whose culture has capital? A critical race theory discussion of community cultural wealth. *Race, Ethnicity & Education, 8*(1), 69–91.

Young, I. M. (1990). *Justice and the politics of difference.* Princeton, NJ: Princeton University Press.

INDEX

NCLB (No Child Left Behind), 27–30, 34
Nosotras, 83–94

O

oppositional behavior, 9, 71, 92
oppression, 7, 9–10, 14, 21–22, 53, 61–76.
   See also discrimination

P

parental engagement
  and academic achievement, 33–34,
    43–44, 144
  with author, 1–7, 22–23, 39–40, 41, 123
  definition of, 23–24, 28, 29
  with Holyoke students, 111–20
  importance of, 33–34
  increase in, 25
  interpretations of, 34–35, 41, 72, 75,
    140–41
  and LatCrit, 70–71
  of Latinx parents
    consejos, 47–49
    as cultural practice, 41–46, 73
    early education vs. college, 84–86, 94,
      100–1
    educación, 44–47, 71–74
    homework. *See* education: in Latinx
      community: and homework
    as invisible, 17, 69, 73, 126
    issues faced, 56, 75
    learning at home, 32, 73
    monitoring, 30, 47, 50–53, 73, 83–84
    as normal, 71–72
    obstacles to, 30, 31, 54–56
    parent/teacher conferences, 23, 50, 73
    and relationships with teachers, 54–56
    respeto, 45–47, 73
    supportive behavior, 50–51, 52, 72–73,
      126

utilizing community, 32
vs. white, 32, 35, 41–44, 54–56, 61,
  71–72, 74, 138
model of, 29
origins of, 24, 139
redefining, 73–74
and school role, 29, 32
with Smith College students, 83–94
with STEM camp students, 126, 128,
  129–30
types of, 29
with UMass students, 97–109
See also college; education
parental involvement. *See* parental engagement
parental resilience, 122–24
PTA (Parent Teacher Association), 23,
  25–31, 34, 72, 114, 138
Puerto Rico
  and author's family, 1, 42, 46
  and cultural contributions, 142
  and educational opportunities, 88, 130
  and Hurricane Maria, 124–25
  Mayor Cruz, 124, 127, 128–29
  and Mount Holyoke, 123–24
  and STEM camp, 11, 124–26
  as study location, 11, 17, 123–35
  as study participants' origin, 123
  and study science fair, 128–29
PWI (Predominantly White Institution),
  22, 68, 81, 92

R

racism
  in education, 15, 61–62, 65–76, 130,
    138–39, 145
  in the law, 62–63
  in society, 1, 14–15, 17, 51, 61–67
  See also discrimination
research steps, 8–12, 82–83, 99–100, 112–13
respeto, 45–47